STEAM AND SAIL: IN BRITAIN AND NORTH AMERICA

STEAM AND SAIL: IN BRITAIN AND NORTH AMERICA

80 Photographs mainly from the National Maritime Museum depicting British and North American Naval, Merchant and Special Purpose vessels of the period of transition from sail to steam

Selected, Introduced and Described by Rear Admiral P W Brock CB DSO, a Trustee, and Basil Greenhill CMG, the Director of the Museum

THE PYNE PRESS

PRINCETON

To
Admiral of the Fleet Sir Algernon Usborne Willis GCB KBE DSO
and to
Captain W. J. Lewis Parker, United States Coastguard (Retd)

First edition

Library of Congress Catalog Card Number 72-95728

SBN 87861-044-8

Printed and bound in Great Britain

Contents

List of Ships

MERCHANT VESSELS

IRIS	1842	Wooden Paddle Steam Packet
GREAT BRITAIN	1843	Iron Screw Steam Passenger Vessel
FULTON	1856	Wooden Paddle Steam Passenger Liner
GREAT EASTERN	1858	Iron Screw and Paddle Steam Passenger Vessel
GIPSY	1859	Iron Screw Steam Packet
AGAMEMNON	1865	Iron Screw Steam Cargo Vessel
NATAL	1866	Iron Screw Steam Passenger and Cargo Vessel
DEUCALION	1872	Iron Screw Steam Cargo Vessel
GERMANIC	1874	Iron Screw Steam Passenger Liner
ANCHORIA	1874	Iron Screw Steam Passenger Liner
DURHAM	1874	Iron Screw Auxiliary Steam Ship
ROME	1881	Iron Screw Steam Passenger Liner
ETRURIA	1884	Steel Screw Steam Passenger Liner
C.R.R. of N.J. No 1	1892	Schooner-Rigged Coal Barge

SPECIAL PURPOSE VESSELS

ICELAND	1872	Wooden Screw Steam Whaler and Sealer
THE STEAM SEALERS		
VANGUARD	1873	Wooden Screw Steam Sealer
HMS, later USS, ALERT	1856	Wooden Screw Steam Sloop, later Exploration Ship
USCGC BEAR	1874	Wooden Screw Steam Sealer, Coastguard Cutter and Exploration Ship
NIMROD	1866	Wooden Screw Steam Sealer
DISCOVERY	1900	Wooden Screw Steam Exploration Ship
ARCTIC	1900	Wooden Screw Steam Exploration Ship
CHUNAR	1845	Iron Paddle Steam River Cargo Vessel
SUNBEAM	1874	Composite Screw Steam Yacht
WATERLILY	1876	Wooden Screw Steam Yacht

THE LAST DAYS OF STEAM AND SAIL

LIEUTENANT GARNIER	1918	Wooden Screw Steam Cargo Vessel
HUSSAR	1931	Steel Screw Diesel Four-Masted Barque Yacht

Sail to steam - the great transition

The period of transition from sail to steam propulsion at sea was a long one. It is of great interest in industrial and maritime history because nothing quite like it had ever happened before or will ever happen again. It covered almost the whole of the nineteenth century. During those hundred years the merchant steamship developed from a wooden, inland waterway vessel propelled by paddle wheels and driven by a crude beam engine, to become a large steel cargo or passenger vessel propelled by twin screws—each driven by compound engines of relatively high efficiency and great reliability. By the end of the period the accommodation offered by the major passenger vessels on the North Atlantic route had reached a very high standard of luxury indeed. Over the period the warship underwent a similar degree of technical change.

But there was a difference between the transition from sail to steam in the Navy and in the merchant shipping industry. In the Navy the process of change was slow but more or less continuous, ending with the total replacement of sail by steam in the last forty years of the century, when no more war vessels were built without power. In the merchant shipping industry the eventual extinction of the sailing vessel, for reasons both economic and social, was probably predictable after the success of the Ocean Steamship Company's compound-engined cargo vessels in the Far Eastern trade in the early 1860s. Nevertheless the next ten years saw a boom in wooden sailing vessel construction, and in the next forty years the sailing vessel was to develop to a degree of efficiency and size not dreamt of in 1860. The great steel four- and five-masted barques of the 1890s, the American wooden four- and five-masted schooners of the same period and the smaller British wooden three-masted schooners and ketches of the 1870s and after were the remarkable products of an age in which the sailing vessel was already obsolescent.

This book covers, with the aid of numerous photographs, some aspects of the use of vessels— naval, merchant, and special purpose—in which steam and sail were used in varying degrees together as means of propulsion. It follows from what has been said above that whereas it covers the whole transition from sail to steam in the Navy it deals only with one part of the more complex story of the transition in merchant shipping. The development of the sailing ship in the age of the camera has already been dealt with by one of the authors with Ann Giffard in *The Merchant Sailing Ship: A Photographic History.*

The Measure of the Problem

We must not be surprised if our forbears did not immediately recognise that steam was the most important maritime development of the nineteenth century. It is necessary to make full allowance for the technical and financial restrictions which beset their development of what was initially a crude and inefficient instrument, with limitations only less marked than its advantages.

Naturally, some conservative opposition had to be overcome, but its strength is commonly exaggerated and its basis is sometimes misunderstood. Pioneers of one decade, convinced like

Job's comforters that they were the people and wisdom would die with them, were apt to become obstructionists in the next. Others might retain a clearer view of the future but lack Lord Fisher's genius for forcing innovations upon believers and doubters alike. History also shows that premature adoption of new ideas could retard real progress more than caution.

Despite much greater knowledge, more advanced scientific aids and greater productive capacity employed under the stimulus of two world wars, a comparable advance in transatlantic air transport in our own time was not achieved overnight or without some doubtful forecasts. As Nevil Shute's autobiography reminds us, twenty years after the Wright brothers' historic flight it was generally agreed that 'aircraft would never be a very suitable vehicle for crossing the Atlantic'. It was another ten years before the revolutionary Douglas DC1 opened new prospects of major development. 'In fact, it was not till 1945 that fare-paying passengers were flown in aeroplanes across the Atlantic on a schedule basis.'

Considering the difficulties that had to be overcome, usually by trial and error, on a tight budget for naval ships and at considerable commercial risk in the merchant shipping industry, the nineteenth-century record in this field is far from discreditable. On the whole there seems less ground for criticising a cautious tempo of development than the prolonged retention of sail in fighting ships towards the end of the period.

The Period of Practical Experiment 1775– c. 1820

Though steam engines invented by pioneers like Newcomen and James Watt were employed in industry ashore throughout most of the eighteenth century, 'steam navigation' only began to show real promise in its last quarter, at much the same moment in France, America and Scotland. In 1788 Robert Burns was a passenger, on Dalswinton Lake, Dumfriesshire, in a small paddle-wheel steamboat owned by his landlord, Patrick Miller, and engined by William Symington. In 1802 Symington's *Charlotte Dundas* was successfully tried as a tug on the Forth and Clyde Canal, only to be vetoed by the canal company, who feared she would damage their banks. Robert Fulton, an American pioneer who attended this trial, gave a demonstration of his own on the Seine a little later, but having failed to interest Britain or France in a submarine, he returned to the United States.

On the Hudson River, plying between New York and Albany, with an engine imported from England, Fulton's *North River Steamboat of Clermont* in 1807 became the world's first commercially profitable steamship. Closely following, John Stevens built and engined the *Phoenix*, which made the first coastal voyage under steam, from Hoboken to Philadelphia. In Scotland Bell's *Comet* began in 1812 a service on the Clyde between Glasgow, Greenock and Helensburgh, and by 1815 there were five steamers on the Thames. Some British engineers were pioneering on the Continent, and in the *Demologos* (later known as *Fulton* or *Fulton the First*) the United States could claim the world's first steam man-of-war. Driven by a paddle wheel working in an internal space on the centreline, with boiler and engine abreast it on opposite sides, she achieved a limited radius at $5\frac{1}{2}$ knots, and mounted a battery of fifteen 32-pounders each side. Owing to the British blockade, the guns had to be hauled overland from Philadelphia and she was too late for the War of 1812-14. She was laid up as a receiving ship until destroyed by an explosion in 1827.

Many accounts of the introduction of steam into the Royal Navy, including that of Sir William Laird Clowes in his massive history, are less than fair to the Admiralty, whose attitude was by no means wholly obstructive. In 1794–5 the Navy Board had backed an initial approach to steam propulsion by the third Earl Stanhope, which came to nothing. In 1815 Lord Melville as First Lord approved fitting an engine in the sloop *Congo* for African exploration, but this proved so heavy and low-powered that it could only be removed for dockyard use ashore. Not long after, on the advice of the elder Brunel, he authorised the experimental trial of a steam ship for towing HM ships out of harbour when the wind was unfavourable. Undeterred by an initial failure, he continued his support until there was sufficient promise to justify providing the Service with steamers of its own for auxiliary purposes.

First Naval Steamships—The Paddle Wheel Era 1820-45

The *Sovereign*, of 202 tons and 80hp, launched on the Thames in 1821, was probably the first steamer built for British government service, but she was a mail packet under Post Office management until 1837 when the Royal Navy took her over and renamed her *Monkey*, having more impressive monarchs on the Navy List. The first steamer built for the Royal Navy was the *Comet*, launched in the royal dockyard at Deptford in 1822. During the next few years, mainly under Lord Melville, the Navy built or acquired a dozen small paddle-wheel steamers for general purposes, including towing and service as mail packets on the overseas routes taken over from the Post Office after the Napoleonic Wars. A claim for the first naval operational service by a steamer has been lodged for the 'steam galliot' *Sea Gull*, a ferry purchased as a despatch vessel for Commodore David Porter USN commanding a squadron suppressing piracy in the West Indies in 1823. The earliest British steamers on operations abroad were the *Lightning* on an expedition to Algiers in 1824, and the *Diana*, acquired in India for service in the First Burma War which also began that year. During the brief interregnum of the Duke of Clarence (soon to be William IV) as Lord High Admiral, HM ships *Lightning*, *Echo* and *Meteor*, commanded by lieutenants appointed with commissions signed by His Royal Highness, were in January 1828, the first steam ships to appear in the quarterly Navy List, marking official recognition of steam as an element of naval power.

By 1830, when Melville finally left the Admiralty, the Royal Navy had gained enough experience to consider building steamers of greater tonnage with something more than a token armament. The legend that Melville blindly resisted progress seems to rest upon the memoirs of Sir John Briggs, a venerable Admiralty civil servant, who stated that when asked by the Colonial Office to provide a mail steamer for the Mediterranean, Melville had replied that national interest and security required the Admiralty to do its utmost to discourage steam navigation. In an Admiralty copy of this engaging but sometimes misleading book, W. G. Perrin, a great and scholarly librarian, has written against that passage: 'This is not true, nor can I find the slightest foundation for it.' Despite his criticism of naval conservatism, however, Briggs, in summing up, asserted that naval weaknesses over much of the Victorian era were 'principally attributable to that ill-judged parsimony that has unhappily characterised the political procedure of the two great parties in the state'.

It should also be remembered that if the rate of progress was not spectacular, neither was the new machinery. The boilers, using salt water, developed little more than atmospheric pressure and had to be blown down quite frequently. They consumed much fuel for very modest power, and the weight of machinery was something like a ton per horse-power. The efficiency of paddle wheels fell off when the vessel was above or below a certain depth of immersion, they were exposed both to weather and enemy fire, and they reduced the number of guns that could be mounted. Steam gave warships tactical mobility but at this stage greatly lowered their strategical radius, to an extent that required the retention of masts and sails except in coast defenders. Sail and steam could sometimes be effectively used together, but when saving fuel under sail alone the paddle wheels had either to be disconnected or to be fixed with the lower blades unshipped, which could be difficult at sea.

Sir James Graham, who became First Lord in 1830, was committed with the Whig party to political reform and naval economy. His senior naval adviser was Vice-Admiral Sir Thomas Hardy, said by Nelson to have been imbued by Providence 'with an intuitive right judgement'. This now ranged him on the side of progress: 'Happen what may, England's duty is to take and keep the lead' was his cry, but he was forced to realise that politics is the art of the possible. The British compromise that followed amounted to little more than a moderate increase in the number and power of steam ships until 1837, when more ambitious programmes, under some fear of France, included paddle-wheel frigates, a number of paddle sloops and from 1840 a few experimental iron ships. In 1837 the Navy took over twenty-six steam packets from the Post Office's cross-Channel service, to provide a steam reserve and steam experience, but not long afterwards the mail service began to be put out to contract, and many Admiralty packets were diverted to other naval purposes.

Amphibious operations on the coast of Syria in 1840, arising out of a revolt against Turkish rule by Egypt with a possibility of French support, gave HM paddle vessels their first real opportunity of operational usefulness. 'I don't know what we should do in this kind of warfare without the steamers, which are a host in themselves', wrote a lieutenant in HMS *Powerful*. Admiral Sir Byam Martin, a notable Comptroller of the Navy from 1815 to 1831 and a great man at all times, looking farther afield now considered that, 'The fleet which is attended by the greatest number of heavy, well-commanded steamers, if judicially conducted, would have the power to inflict merciless wounds with impunity, so that a first-rate may be bled to death, if I may so say, without receiving a wound in return.'

In the United States Navy, post-war reaction and retrenchment gave little encouragement after 1815 to the pioneering spirit that had produced the first *Fulton*. Fifteen years later, 'The young and progressive officers of the war were now becoming the old and ultra-conservative officers of a peacetime navy.' It was the Secretary of the Navy, Mahlon Dickerson, who in 1834 called the attention of the Board of Navy Commissioners to an Act of Congress of 1816 which had authorised the construction of three experimental 'steam-batteries' and directed them to produce one. He did, however, have the professional advice and support of Commander Matthew Galbraith Perry, who in December 1837 commissioned the second *Fulton*. Despite some technical limitations, to be expected in such a project, Captain Perry showed her to such advantage that on 3 March 1839 Congress authorised three more steamers. Having seen recent developments in England and France, Perry, with suitable technical assistance, played an important part in designing the paddle-wheel frigates *Mississippi* and *Missouri*. Launched in 1842, they were equal, if not superior to, HMS *Terrible* of 1845, regarded as Britain's finest frigate of this type. H. I. Chapelle, historian of the development of the American sailing navy, says: 'These ships really marked the beginning of the decline of importance of sailing men-of-war, though it was twenty years more before the last die-hards would recognise the supremacy of the steamship.'

British paddle-wheel ships, as shown in the Navy List of 1845, included 12 frigates, over 30 sloops and more than 100 miscellaneous types, but this was the peak of their brief era in the Royal Navy. The screw propeller, with other innovations in engineering, weapons and ship construction, soon confined naval use of the paddle wheel to ships intended for special purposes.

The Merchant Paddle Steamer

Given the uncertainty, unreliability and gross discomfort of the sailing vessel as a vehicle for passenger transport it is only natural that it was as passenger vessels on rivers and short sea routes around the coasts of Britain and the United States that steamers first became established as profitable earning units of the merchant shipping industry. Like those of warships their engines absorbed great quantities of coal in relation to the distance steamed, their paddles were inefficient as a propelling device at sea and they could not carry enough fuel to steam very far, but they could offer regular, fast services for short distances. In 1813 there were nine passenger-carrying steam vessels working around New York city, six out of Philadelphia. In 1815 there were steamers on Chesapeake Bay and in 1817 a service was set up between Charleston, South Carolina and Savannah, Georgia. By mid-1815 a steamer had steamed from the Clyde to Liverpool, and a year later a regular service across the Irish Sea was started to and from Holyhead. In 1815 also the Clyde-built *Thames* steamed to London from the Clyde on a historic passage via Dublin and round Land's End.

A small boom in steamship building took place in some parts of Britain when at the end of the Napoleonic Wars a period of industrial expansion led to the relatively ready availability of the materials and facilities for engine building. There were nearly forty steamers operating on the Clyde by 1820. By 1822 the *James Watt* was in regular service between London and Leith and soon every obvious route had its paddle packet. A cross-Channel service was inaugurated and tugs began to appear at the major ports. By 1827, according to Robin Craig, the merchant shipping historian, there were 225 steamships registered as of British ports under the current Merchant Shipping Act. But ten years later, when there were over 700 United States steamships, mostly on inland waterways, there were still only 624 registered in Britain. The reason was, of course that the short service routes around Britain on which steamships were economic were soon saturated and it was to be a long time before steamships could be profitably operated on even the most lucrative of ocean passenger routes—the crossing of the North Atlantic. At the same time the paddle steamer was playing a vital part in the opening up of the West in the United States and in the development of fast coastal services in sheltered waters.

Experiments with steamships on ocean routes started very early—sometimes by way of delivery voyages. The steam auxiliary wooden full-rigged ship *Savannah* crossed from Savannah, Georgia, to Liverpool in 1819. She was followed in 1821–2 by the *Rising Star*, a British vessel which made the crossing well to the South but in a westerly direction while in process of delivery to owners in Chile. In 1824 the lug-rigged *Enterprise* steamed for 62 out of the 100 days she took to reach Calcutta from Britain and at full speed under steam in fine weather she could, according to some authorities, make 6 to 7 knots, which after all was still the best speed of some tramp steamers a century later. In 1831 the *Sarah Jane* made a steam-assisted passage to Australia. Two years later the *Cape Breton*, built at Blackwall earlier in the same year, made a passage from Plymouth to Sydney, Nova Scotia and thus for the first time a steam-assisted vessel made the most difficult of all crossings, the East to West passage of the North Atlantic. In 1838 a regular trans-Atlantic service in vessels propelled almost entirely by their steam engines was started by the *Great Western* which was, of course, the first of the three great steamships with which Isambard Kingdom Brunel was closely associated. Made commercially possible by a mail subsidy, she marked the beginning of a new era for steam at sea. In comparison with the accommodation in sailing vessels she offered her passengers luxury and, for the first time, the passenger became an important commercial asset to be cultivated and treated as such.

The usefulness of the screw may have been perceived even earlier than by Archimedes in the 3rd century BC, but the first practical experiments in applying it to ship propulsion were nearly contemporary with the steam engine, and it was rather later in undergoing important trials. In 1836 Frances Pettit Smith, an English farmer, obtained a patent for his screw propeller just before a different type was patented by Captain John Ericsson, a Swedish army captain who had come to London. The latter demonstrated his in 1837 by towing the Admiralty barge, with the Senior Naval Lord and other dignitaries, from Somerset House to Blackwall and back at something like ten knots, but apparently he failed to convince Captain William Symonds, RN, Surveyor of the Navy, that on a larger scale the screw would not interfere with steering. The appointment of a naval officer with little more than a penchant for ship-designing to a post customarily held by a Master Shipwright of great practical experience had naturally aroused criticism. Symonds had, however, made a promising start but it was unfortunate that his open aversion to steam made him reluctant to progress in this direction. In regard to the screw, his view was then shared by many engineers, but with greater foresight Captain Stockton, USN, promising Ericsson that 'We'll make your name ring on the Delaware', secured his talents for the New World.

In England, Smith's propeller in the steamship *Archimedes* proved so successful in trials in 1839–40 that Brunel's *Great Britain* was modified to adopt it. Also the Admiralty, despite Symonds, ordered the conversion of HMS *Rattler*, building as a paddle sloop, to try the screw against similar ships. At the same time, HMS *Bee*, a small wooden vessel, was built with both screw and paddle wheels for instructional purposes. By a narrow margin HMS *Dwarf*, ex-*Mermaid*, a small iron steamer purchased in 1843, became the first screw ship in service in the Royal Navy.

The screw introduced problems in both engineering and ship design, and it is interesting to find Admiral Sir George Cockburn, represented by Briggs as the arch-enemy of progress, writing in 1844: 'As soon as we shall have decided on the best shape and the best propeller, we shall certainly advance our number of steam warships as fast, if not faster, than (the French) can; and we have already many plans for keeping the machinery below the water.' Comparative trials between the *Rattler* and the paddle sloop *Alecto* in 1845, including the famous tug-of-war with the ships lashed stern to stern, were an important, though not final, factor in deciding in favour of the screw. By 1850, however, it had ousted the paddle wheel in nearly all new types of warship, and in 1852 HMS *Agamemnon* of 91 guns was launched as the first ship of the line designed for the screw but still fully rigged. For some years, however, the conversion of existing sailing ships to auxiliary steam continued, as the quickest means of keeping pace with the French.

Captain R. F. Stockton USN, having persuaded Ericsson that his future lay in America, followed up by convincing the Secretary of the Navy that the third ship which Congress had authorised in 1839 should be not a 'side-wheeler' but a screw ship. He then summoned Ericsson to prepare detailed plans under his general supervision. The *Princeton*, as she was named, after Stockton's home town, slightly anticipated HMS *Rattler*'s conversion to screw propulsion and was potentially a much more formidable fighting ship. Unhappily, she proved a great disappointment, for all Ericsson's customary ingenuity. On her trial trip the bursting of a 12 in gun of Stockton's design killed the Secretary of State, the Secretary of the Navy, two congressmen and an officer, and wounded Stockton himself, amongst a number of others. It also broke up the partnership between Stockton and Ericsson, who undertook no further work for the Navy until the Civil War. The *Princeton* served in the Mexican War of 1846–7 but after a short cruise in the Mediterranean she was condemned by survey in 1849. An attempt to 're-build' her was also fruitless.

Another pioneering step was taken by the United States Navy in 1842 when Congress was induced to grant $250,000 towards the first ironclad warship for any navy. She was to be built by private enterprise. 'But this also proved to be a false start. Work on the Stevens Battery, as this vessel came to be known, dragged along from year to year, and finally came to a stop.' Further substantial injections of both government and private funds failed to get her under way. Slow building is always expensive building, and often abortive. Disappointed with pioneering, the United States Navy built two more large paddle-wheel frigates, the *Powhatan* and *Susquehanna*, before making a substantial but conventional advance in authorising six first-class screw frigates, fully rigged, in 1854.

An important development of this period was that of a type of propeller which could be disengaged from its shaft and lifted out of the water so as to eliminate its drag when sailing. The successful application of this device led to the era of 'up funnel and down screw'—the orders said to have been given when starting engines and going over to propulsion at least partly by steam power. Lifting screws were used in some early merchant ships with steam power, like the *Calcutta* built in 1852 and running to India and Australia for the General Screw Steam Shipping Co Ltd. On board her a passenger wrote, 'Yesterday the wind freshened so that they took up the screw and the ship went on under canvas. I thought it a much pleasanter motion, but we rolled about a good deal more. . . .' Lifting screws were used much later in special-purpose vessels which spent periods of time working in ice, the screw being lifted from time to time to protect it from damage. Another important device of the steam-and-sail era, for use when vessels were being driven by both sails and steam, was the variable pitch propeller, which, controlled from the deck, enabled the engines to work at maximum advantage under different conditions of load.

Two developments affecting warships rather than merchantmen first became significant during this period. The first was the provision of explosive-filled shells, instead of solid shot, for some of the guns of a ship's battery. Hitherto the use of shells at sea had mainly been confined to mortar vessels bombarding shore positions: for a fleet action at close range the fuses seemed unreliable, and accidental explosions showed that shells could be a potential danger on board. When trials convinced the French of their efficiency, however, the Royal Navy had to follow suit; and the demand for a bursting charge heavier than could be carried in a 32 lb (6.3 in) spherical projectile led to the introduction of some 8 in and 10 in guns, primarily for firing shells. The second important, though temporary, development was that gunnery trials against iron plating cast doubts on its suitability for warship construction, just after the initial objections to it had been overridden. These had included the obvious fact that iron did not float, the belief that it punctured more easily than wood, its more rapid fouling by weed and barnacles than a copper-sheathed wooden hull, and the compass deviation it produced. There were answers to these difficulties and in 1845 five iron frigates were building. Unfortunately, the jagged holes and fragmentation of both projectiles and plating that occurred in trials up to 1850 caused the frigates to be converted for other purposes. We may now regard the trials as having shown indifferent quality of metal, but both the French and American navies temporarily accepted the British view that iron would not do for a man-of-war.

In regard to propulsion, however, Admiral Sir E. R. Fremantle, recalling his midshipman's time in HMS *Queen*, wearing the flag of Sir William Parker 'the last of Nelson's captains', in the Mediterranean in 1849–52, wrote: 'I will only remark how reluctant we were to acknowledge the power of steam and that the poetry of sails and sailing ships was leaving us; and though I shared fully the prejudices against steam and steamers at that time—"smoke jacks" we called them, pitying the midshipmen who had to serve in them—I could not help seeing that with the advent of the screw propeller the days of sailing ships were numbered.

The Screw-Driven Merchant Steamship 1843-65

As has already been said, the paddle steamer had many disadvantages as a passenger and cargo carrier except for short passages in tidal or shallow waters. In the great side-lever engines which were used in many British vessels massive weights moved up and down, stopping and reversing on every stroke and setting up stresses in the structure of the machinery and the hull which carried it. The paddle was a most inefficient means of propulsion at sea and far too susceptible to damage in heavy weather. The paddle tug was to remain an important feature of the maritime scene until the twentieth century and crucial to the later development of the big merchant sailing vessel. Here steam was the handmaid of sail and the new technology came to the aid of the old. Shallow-draft short-range excursion and ferry paddle steamers continued to be built for service when very shallow draft was required, as when running a scheduled service to piers and wharves in tidal waters. But as competitive carriers on ocean routes the paddle steamers were greatly handicapped.

There were also grave difficulties in the way of the development of screw-driven merchant steamships. Ordinary wooden merchant ships were not as massively built as war vessels. They had to be able to carry bulky cargoes and therefore they could not be so heavily constructed. Also, they had to represent an economic investment and consequently their building costs had to be kept down. But unless a wooden vessel was built to be massively strong the stresses set up in her hull by screw propulsion led to her leaking and ageing rapidly. The necessary material for building relatively light strong hulls, iron, was not readily available in the quantities and sizes required for building big merchant ships until after the construction of the *Great Britain*. The slow-running engines of the period, working at the low steam pressures available, were not really suited to screw propulsion. So it was not until the 1850s that screw steamers began to appear in any numbers. Big paddle steamers continued on the North Atlantic run and continued to be built until the mid–1850s. Even then, because of the inefficiency of their simple engines, the limited amount of fuel they could carry in relation to consumption and the scarcity of bunkering facilities, screw steamers tended to be operated as auxiliaries. They were fully rigged sailing vessels with steam engines which were used at the predictable periods on long ocean voyages when sailing conditions were not favourable. Only on the North Atlantic route could fully powered steamers hope to compete directly with sailing vessels and the *City of Glasgow* of the late 1840s is often spoken of as the first really successful ocean steamship. She was able to pay her way in competition with the North Atlantic sailing packets without a government mail subsidy.

Three products of nineteenth-century engineering and industrial development had to be brought together before a steamship could compete freely on many world routes with contemporary sailing vessels. First, iron in large dimensions and at reasonable prices had to be readily available. Then the screw propeller had to be developed to a relatively high level of efficiency. Finally, the compound engine with its greater efficiency and smaller fuel consumption had to be applied to the driving of the propeller and this, of course, meant higher pressures than were possible with the boilers of the first half of the nineteenth century. These technical developments could only be utilised effectively when a reasonable pattern of bunkering facilities had been established on the principal trade routes on which steamers could hope to compete with sail. The compound engine was, of course, the key to the success of the merchant steamship and its manufacture in Britain was one of the important factors in British industrial, commercial and in some degree political ascendancy in the last thirty years of the nineteenth century. The widespread establishment

16

of bunkering stations at key points under British control made possible its effective utilisation by freeing space in vessels for the carriage of economically viable quantities of cargo.

A major turning point was the launching by the Ocean Steamship Company, parent of the Blue Funnel Line, of the *Agamemnon*, the *Ajax* and the *Achilles*, all built by Scott & Company of Greenock in 1865. The successful use of these vessels in the China trade from 1865 onwards was a pointer to the end of the merchant sailing ship as a vehicle of general ocean commerce. Not only did the vessels incorporate considerable technical developments, but their owners applied managerial techniques designed to utilise the potentialities of this new breed of ocean-going ship. The success of these vessels marked the beginning of the end of the era of steam and sail, for until now all steam vessels, however heavily powered, were of necessity rigged almost as heavily as contemporary sailing vessels. The new compound engines were rapidly developed to a point at which sails were no longer necessary to economise on fuel in normal operations and much less likely to be needed in emergencies. The final abandonment of sails in large merchant vessels followed the introduction of twin screws.

The handling of sailing ships at sea, working or fighting, was one of the most complex of the more widely used skills developed by man. The really successful handling of a big sailing vessel was something only a few could hope to achieve, and then only after years of extremely hard experience. It was natural, therefore, that this skill was a long time in being abandoned and that even the most powerful steamships continued to be handled by masters and mates trained in sailing vessels in a manner which made the maximum use of their sails as long as they had them. A log kept on board the pioneer Cunarder, the wooden paddle steamer *Britannia*, on her first Atlantic crossing in 1840, despite the fact that she steamed all the way and had adequate power, contains numerous references not only to the handling of sails but also the sending down of upper masts and yards in bad weather in the manner adopted in contemporary sailing vessels. But one of the most significant entries refers to a head wind and reports that all sails were taken in and the upper yards and masts sent down, no doubt to reduce windage while the *Britannia*, unlike a sailing vessel, continued straight ahead on her course. As late as 1880 the Royal Mail Steam Packet Company's *Neva* had square sails set for 803 hours out of the 1,008 hours of a typical passage.

The development of iron and later steel for shipbuilding had another very significant effect. The new materials were not at first available in quantity at economic prices in North America and both the United States and Canada were entering a phase of looking to their own vast internal development potential. Enterprise and capital turned from shipping and in 1870 the United States had only 192,544 tons of steam shipping registered for foreign trade while Britain had more than six times as much. This difference is not fully reflected in this book in which more than a third of the vessels described in the main photographs were either of the United States Navy or built or owned in the United States or Canada.

The Growing Power of Steam and the Armoured Capital Ship 1854-70

The need for steam was soon made clear when England and France went to Turkey's aid in the war with Russia in 1854. Though this was generally called the Crimean War, its naval activity extended also to the Baltic and, in a small way, to the White Sea and the Pacific. Since the Russian fleet was too weak to meet the Allies in battle and refrained from commerce raiding, naval operations were largely amphibious and coastal, in waters where the manoeuvrability of steamers was invaluable. In the Baltic in 1854, most of the British ships had steam at command but most of the French had not, and they were often a drag on proceedings despite a willing spirit. In the Black Sea sail predominated in both fleets that year, and off Odessa and Sebastopol British men-of-war were for the last time in action under sail. They included the frigate *Arethusa*, designed by Symonds and commanded by his son. The inclusion of only a single steamer, the paddle sloop *Virago*, in a joint squadron sent across the Pacific to attack Petropavlovsk was one reason why an ill-conducted expedition came to a very broken conclusion. After the war, the First Lord, Sir Charles Wood (later Lord Halifax) said that sailing ships of war 'ought almost to be left out of consideration'; a year later he strengthened this to 'Sailing vessels, though useful in time of peace, would never again be employed in war.'

Second in importance to this lesson was the impression made by the shell fire of the Russian batteries at Sebastopol. It was perhaps more moral than material, for the damage and casualties sustained were not very heavy by the standards of either Napoleonic or modern hard-fought war, and did not stir the Admiralty to immediate action. It did, however, create a demand for protection sufficient to induce the French to build some armoured floating batteries which stood up well to enemy fire at Kinburn in 1855. Their steam power gave them only about four knots, so they required a tow for any strategical movement.

In 1858 France took the next step, to an armoured heavy ship, which America had unsuccessfully attempted in the 'Stevens battery' of the 1840s. France's brilliant constructor Dupuy de Lôme designed *La Gloire*, an armoured wooden-hulled, well-armed ship, on frigate lines, as the first of a new fleet to challenge British supremacy. Admiral Sir Baldwin Walker, succeeding Symonds as Surveyor of the Navy but without his responsibility for detailed ship-design, had hitherto held that a policy of gradual evolution was the proper course for the strongest Navy with a greater capital investment in ships of conventional type. But in view of this new development he now urged 'as a matter not only of expediency but of absolute necessity' a competitive British advance.

This resulted in the splendid ironclads *Warrior* and *Black Prince*, whose graceful lines contrasted strongly with what an American officer called 'the sullen, low-browed, graceless aspect' of the *Gloire*. Designed by Isaac Watts, Chief Constructor of the Navy, advised by Scott Russell, a private shipbuilder with experience in iron construction, they were iron-hulled, with a 4½ in armour belt backed by heavy oak to protect their vitals. They were ship-rigged with sails of moderate dimensions, and had telescopic funnels and a hoisting screw. In most respects they were considered superior to the *Gloire*, except by those for whom the far-off hills are always greener. They had to be built by contract, since the royal dockyards were not yet able to cope with iron ships of their great size, whereas British industry as a whole was better equipped than the French.

When the *Warrior* was laid down in 1859 the last five purely sailing ships-of-the-line in full commission, all flagships on foreign stations where coal was not yet readily available, had either reached or were approaching the end of their active service; and the *Victoria* of 121 guns about to be launched at Portsmouth was the last three-decked steam ship-of-the-line that would ever be completed for sea. Displacing 6,960 tons, she was nearing the limits of wooden warship construction, as indeed were some frigates built in 1856–9 to match the six powerful American steam frigates, including the *Niagara* and *Merrimack* (or *Merrimac*) authorised in 1854. Besides having limited longitudinal strength if heavily loaded, wooden hulls suffered from the vibration of the machinery, and the best building timber had been in short supply in Britain since 'eighteen-hundred-and-wartime' in the long struggle with Napoleon. Consequently resumption of iron shipbuilding was warmly received by 'the movement party' as advocates of progress had once been termed. Thereafter a few wooden ships were given an armour belt as the quickest expedient to overtake the French programme, but the building of unarmoured wooden screw ships-of-the-line ceased in 1862. HMS *Endymion*, the last wooden screw frigate, was launched in 1865. Smaller wooden screw ships continued in diminishing numbers until 1874 when the screw corvettes *Sapphire* and *Diamond* were the last wooden ships from Devonport and Sheerness, respectively.

The need for steam having been established and better-quality iron having regained respectability, weapons and armour provided the designer's major problems for the next decade. Guns built up of wrought iron and steel were abolishing the limits imposed by cast iron, while rifling and breech-loading promised greater accuracy and ease of loading. Between 1865 and 1871 the naval gun developed from a 7in weapon weighing $6\frac{1}{2}$ tons to one of 12in diameter and 35 tons weight, producing demands for thicker armour. This double increase in weight meant a drastic reduction in the number of guns that could be carried: the more powerful the ship, the fewer her guns now became. This made the time-honoured system of assessing the strength of a ship primarily by her number of guns quite meaningless, and for some time the classification of warships was extremely confused.

On some important questions of general design, the Admiralty did not find that confusion was materially relieved by war experience, whether British or vicarious. With one minor exception to be mentioned shortly, there were no fleet actions, and the only experience in the defence of seaborne trade was that afforded by the operations of a few Confederate raiders. The Russian War, China in 1856–60 and the American Civil War tended to focus attention on confined waters and coastal attack and defence. Shallow draught thus became a more important factor than engineering or manoeuvrability in the introduction of twin screws in British men-of-war. In action with Japanese forts at Kagoshima in 1863 the Armstrong breech-loading guns which the Royal Navy had adopted with unusual alacrity in 1860 seemed so prone to accident that the heavier types were discarded even more hastily. Herr Krupp's breech-loaders, it may be remarked, were equally disappointing in Prussia's Seven Weeks' War with Austria in 1866, but he was allowed to correct mistakes. The Admiralty, on the other hand, went over to rifled muzzle-loading guns. With the short guns and quick-burning powder then in use these were probably as effective for the time being, but not for long, since slow-burning propellants were soon becoming available to give higher muzzle velocity in a longer gun.

At Hampton Roads in March 1862 Ericsson's *Monitor*, whose turret on a very low armoured hull was compared to 'a tin can on a shingle' or 'a cheesebox on a raft', engaged the Confederate ironclad *Virginia*, improvised from the hull of the United States steam frigate *Merrimac(k)*, in the world's first duel between armoured ships. Ericsson had chosen the name *Monitor* in the expectation or hope that she might enlighten backward folk like the British Admiralty, but perhaps what the action revealed most clearly was that in battle weapons may have limitations not evident in practices and trials, and that for the moment the gun had not mastered armour. The *Monitor* later foundered in the open sea off Cape Hatteras—another kind of lesson. Nevertheless, her single turret had held off the more heavily armed *Virginia* and checked her offensive, thereby supporting Captain Cowper Coles RN, who had been pressing the advantages of turrets upon the Admiralty.

In coast defence ships, turrets clearly provided an answer to the problem of giving a few heavy guns the greatest possible arcs of fire. Unhappily Coles was bent upon extending their use to a capital ship which would combine a low hull, offering only a small, well-armoured target, with a full rig. Rejecting the view of the Admiralty technicians that such a ship would not have the stability to carry sail, Coles conducted a publicity campaign that with the support of *The Times* and the First Lord of the Admiralty forced the Controller into accepting a remarkable compromise—HMS *Captain*, to be built by contract under Coles's general guidance, while they played a Pontius Pilate role. This was a sorry business from the start to its end on the night of 6 September 1870, when the *Captain* capsized in half a gale off Finisterre. Of all those concerned, the only ones who could be congratulated were her Gunner and seventeen men who survived in the ship's launch.

As an example of a dubious lesson from history, the Battle of Lissa in 1866, in which the Austrians defeated a stronger Italian fleet, greatly encouraged those who thought that ramming was likely to be the principal means of attack at sea, having failed to note that the *Re d'Italia* was disabled and stopped when rammed by Tegethoff's flagship. Inadequate leadership and training were the most important factors in the Italian defeat, and ramming was only very occasionally successful in the War between the States, but for nearly forty years most battleships and cruisers had some form of ram bow.

In 1861 it was fortunate for the United States Navy that, 'more by good luck than good management' wrote Mahan, 'In the decade before the Civil War began there had been built eighteen or twenty new steamships, admirably efficient for their day, and with armaments of an advanced and powerful type. Upon them fell the principal brunt of the naval fighting that ensued. These ships, and particularly those of the *Brooklyn* class, were the backbone of Farragut's fleet throughout all his actions, even in the last at Mobile in 1864.' At the start of the war the United States Navy had mustered 34 steamers and 48 sailing ships. By 1865 it had increased to 63 armoured steam vessels on *Monitor* lines, 112 screw and paddle-wheel ships of more conventional type and 12 steam tugs and service craft, making 177 in all, together with nearly 500 purchased vessels. Apart from the monitors which, having no sail, are outside the scope of this book, the only significant development in ship design was an attempt to produce really fast cruisers which, as potential commerce raiders, might discourage any foreign power from intervening in the war; but the danger had passed before they were ready. In post-war comparative trials of this batch the *Wampanoag* (soon renamed *Florida*) showed most promise, but by then the Navy Department, with post-war retrenchment in force, was more inclined to revert to old ways, including maximum use of sail for cruising, than to explore new ones.

'A museum of experiments', Tirpitz's description of the young German Navy of a decade later, applied equally well to the British battle fleet of 1870. A tight economic rein had been grudgingly eased to keep ahead of France, but technical advance could only proceed in stages, and by trial and error. The way ahead was not yet clear, but in retrospect one can see some substantial progress. As Admiral Ballard pointed out, at this mid-point of Queen Victoria's reign the British battleship was half way through a transformation from an entirely wooden, wind-propelled vessel, armed only with a large number of light, hand-worked guns firing through ports in her side, into a metal structure, steam-driven, and armed not only with a comparatively few heavy, power-worked guns above deck but with underwater weapons also. In 1870 the battle fleet included both wood and iron hulls; though steam was dominant, sail still remained in all seagoing ships. Some of them mounted both the old hand-worked guns internally and the new heavy, power-worked weapons above the weather deck, and Whitehead's locomotive torpedo was just about to be adopted. Smaller ships were less advanced. Armour had been tried but found unprofitable for them. A few wooden corvettes and gun vessels had still to be launched but a wood skin was now combined with an iron frame in a growing number of 'composite-built' unarmoured ships of moderate dimensions. The speed of cruising ships relative to that of the capital ship left a good deal to be desired, but that was hard to avoid at this stage of engineering development.

The End of Steam and Sail in Merchant Vessels

The use of sail in large merchant steamships was rapidly abandoned after the introduction of twin screws, in the 1880s. With the development of more reliable engines and the provision of bunkering stations on main trade routes even single screw ships were stripped of their yards and rigging. The first Lord Runciman wrote in his autobiography *Before The Mast—And After* of his experiences in the mid-eighties with the first ship he owned: 'Waste in every direction was made impossible. The vessel had four square sail yards. This meant gear, sails, ropes, yards, paints, labour, and retarding speed during contrary winds, without obtaining anything like compensating advantages with fair winds. All superfluity of this kind was abolished. . . . Whoever puts squaresails on a steamer now?'

The Passing of Naval Sail—1870 onwards

Misgivings raised by the loss of HMS *Captain* led in 1871 to a Committee on Designs under Lord Dufferin. It was to consider ship design in general, and in particular Reed's *Devastation* on the slip at Portsmouth which was to be the first capital ship without masts and sails. The saving in weight and manpower arising from this allowed her coal to be doubled, giving her an oceanic endurance, and to be twin-screwed, providing an insurance against complete mechanical breakdown. Her freeboard, though modest, was greater than the *Captain*'s and adequate for a 'mastless' ship. She had bow and stern turrets with arcs of fire unimpeded by rigging. A committee including a number of naval officers could hardly be expected to be unanimous, but it was generally agreed that 'the *Devastation* class represents in its broad features the first-class fighting ship of the immediate future' and a large majority favoured giving up sail. Unfortunately, the minority commanded an influence that unduly prolonged its survival, certainly as far as the capital ship was concerned, since she was now about to be given a substantial increase in steaming radius through the compound engine using higher-pressure steam expansively, as recommended by the committee.

The last British armoured ship to have full ship rig with a single screw was the small ironclad *Nelson*, launched in 1875, which in 1878 was classed as the first 'armoured cruiser'. HMS *Inflexible*, launched in 1876 but not completed until 1881 after many alterations, received a brig rig primarily to allow her to compete with other ships in sail drill, with arrangements to allow it to be jettisoned quickly if action was imminent. No more 'masted' battleships were laid down, but the new category of armoured cruiser in 1883 included the *Imperieuse* and *Warspite* which were completed with a brig rig. Trials proved this to be so useless that it was removed and replaced by a single 'military' mast amidships.

The diehards' argument that sail should be retained in case of breakdown was weakened when, during a period of strained relations with Russia in 1885, HMS *Monarch*'s machinery refused duty between Alexandria and Malta with the Commander-in-Chief, Mediterranean, on board, and she made such limited progress under sail that a search had to be made to locate her and tow her into Malta. It was not until 1891, however, that 'the Great Brig', HMS *Temeraire*, returned from the Mediterranean to pay off, leaving the *Bellerophon* in the West Indies as the last 'masted' British battleship in full commission.

The value attached to sail training for young officers and ratings for long sustained a 'flying' or detached squadron which carried out extended cruises mainly under sail. One unexpected critic had been Captain C. C. Penrose Fitzgerald, recognised as a masterly handler of sailing ships and craft, who as flag captain to the Earl of Clanwilliam on this squadron's world cruise with two royal princes in 1880 was bold enough to suggest that the best jockeys were not trained on camels. The squadron remained in being nevertheless until late in 1899, when it would have been an easy prey had a European power gone to war in support of the South African republics.

It has already been mentioned that after the Civil War the American Navy began to drift back into the habits and routine of pre-war days. The Navy Board was by no means solely to blame for this, for in addition to the post-war reaction against all things military, inevitable in a democracy, the need for reconstruction in the South competed with the claims of development in the West. As has been said, the American merchant marine had seriously declined, from wartime losses to Confederate raiders and transfers to foreign registry as well as from a surprising apathy towards 'steam navigation' and iron ships. This removed one argument for a strong navy. Politics and vested interests diverted money that would have been better spent on new construction into extravagant maintenance of outworn and outmoded men-of-war. The 1870s were a most lean and depressing period for the United States Navy.

Between the end of the war and 1880, barely a score of new ships were laid down, the largest being the wooden screw frigate *Trenton* of 3,900 tons. The others included fourteen wooden screw corvettes and sloops, three iron gun vessels and two small iron torpedo rams. All had sail but the last two, and were of strictly conventional design. The autobiography of Admiral Robley D. Evans recalls that during a time of tension with Spain in 1873:

> The force assembled at Key West was the best, and indeed about all, we had. We had no stores or storehouses to speak of at this so-called base of supplies, and if it had not been so serious it would have been laughable to see our condition. We remained there several weeks, making faces at the Spaniards ninety miles away at Havana, while two modern vessels of war would have done us up in thirty minutes.

Some years later the future Admiral of the Navy, George Dewey, then a senior commander, was appointed to command a second-rate sloop of 1861:

> . . . a relic of a past epoch of naval warfare . . . as out of date as the stagecoach. Naval science had gone rapidly and we had stood still. While Europe was building armored battleships and fast cruisers, we were making no additions to our navy. We had no sea-going commerce to protect. With the coming of steel hulls and steam this had all passed to England and France, and the rising seapower, the German Empire. Therefore no one had any interest in the Navy. Our antiquated men-of-war had become the laughing stock of the nation. Their only possible utility was as something that would float for officers and men to cruise in, in time of peace, and be murdered in by a few broadsides in time of war. We had appropriations only for running expenses and repairs, none for building new ships. Italy, Spain and Holland were each stronger on the sea than the United States.

In 1881, however, the turning point was reached when a new President took office with a majority in both branches of Congress, financial and industrial recovery in flood, and a growing demand for naval reform. On the material side, this entailed disposing of the ageing wooden ships of the Old Navy and building the New One. The former were phased out by strictly limiting the money to be devoted to repair. The latter began in 1883 when Congress, after considering the recommendations of two advisory boards, authorised the construction of three cruisers, the *Atlanta*, *Boston*, and *Chicago* and a despatch vessel, *Dolphin*. All had sail, but Robley Evans as a member of one of the boards obtained a decision that they should be steel-hulled, and both materially and psychologically they were a major advance. In *The Steam Navy of the United States*, Bennett says: 'It is not unfashionable now to harshly criticize that Board for not knowing everything that experience has taught since, but its work speaks well enough in results for the thoroughness and earnest endeavour of the members to do the best possible for the Service in the beginning of its new life.' It was the foundation of the mighty fleets of the two world wars.

The last American man-of-war of any size to be completed with masts and sails was the cruiser *Newark* in 1890. Most of the ships so fitted discarded their sails during the next decade, but a small training ship with full ship rig was built for the Naval Academy in 1900 and carried out practice cruises with the midshipmen as the *Chesapeake* until 1904, then renamed *Severn* in 1905–07.

This corresponded fairly well with the Royal Navy's policy, except that a few British smaller ships intended for foreign service in distant waters with limited facilities carried a barquentine rig into the twentieth century. It is often said that the disappearance of HMS *Condor* somewhere off Cape Flattery in the North Pacific in 1901 ended British naval sail, but she may have been in collision with an American merchant ship lost at that time, and a few vestiges of sail lingered on. In the Channel, training brigs for boys continued until 1903–4, and HMS *Racer* still longer for young officers. Some cruisers retained fore-and-aft steadying sails for a time. In 1904 HMS *Grafton*, recalled from the Pacific under Fisher's policy of concentration at home, got hers out of a locker and hoisted them 'for fun' crossing the Bay of Biscay, claiming an extra knot or so from them.

Sail had had a long reign and produced great seamen, and as late as 1930 the First Lord did not lack support when he proposed to reintroduce a substantial measure of sail training. There is little doubt, however, that Lord Chatfield was right in believing that it could not profitably be resurrected on a useful scale under modern conditions. One must remain grateful for the enthusiasm for boat sailing that is still widely evident in the Services and elsewhere today.

Naval Vessels

HMS *Salamander 1832-83*

Wooden Paddle-Wheel Sloop, 2nd Class*

The *Salamander, Phoenix, Dee, Rhadamanthus* and *Medea*, varying somewhat in size and horsepower, were early attempts by four different Master Shipwrights to design a paddle-wheel man-of-war more formidable than a gun vessel.

HMS *Salamander* was designed by Mr Seaton and when launched on 16 May 1832 at Sheerness Dockyard she was assessed as being of 818 tons burthen (or Builder's Measurement). Her engines were of 220 nominal horse power, giving her a speed of 7 knots. In later years her Navy List displacement was 1,380 tons and her indicated horse power 506. She was originally armed with two 10in 84cwt pivot guns and two 32-pounder carronades on common (truck) carriages. Two more carronades were added later. Her cost was £32,179, exclusive of stores. In common with all the Navy's early paddle-wheelers, her engines were of the side-lever type. This was an inverted form of the 'walking-beam' engine that was a familiar sight on North American waterways well into this century, but its overhead lever would have multiplied the disadvantages of paddle-wheels in a seagoing fighting ship. A perfect example of a pair of side-lever engines can be seen working in the paddle tug *Reliant* at the National Maritime Museum. The *Salamander's* barque rig gave her the strategic mobility denied by her uneconomic machinery. When under sail alone it was customary in these ships either to fix the paddle wheels and unship their lower blades or, if design permitted, to disconnect the engine and free-wheel. Both sail and paddle could often be used.

Under Commander S. C. Dacres, the *Salamander* in 1836–7 saw active service on the north coast of Spain, assisting the cause of the young Queen Isabella against her uncle, Don Carlos, who disputed her succession. The *Salamander* often carried troops—one of the functions foreseen for these ships—as well as providing gunfire support and landing her own ship's company.

Though the screw made paddle-wheelers obsolescent as major war vessels in the later 1840s, many continued to give years of useful service in other roles. The *Salamander* took part in the Second Burma War in 1852, and in 1865 was surveying the coast of Queensland. From 1870 she was allocated to coasting services, transporting stores and the like from one royal dockyard to another, until paid off in 1875 and noted as 'not worth repair'. She was sold in 1883 after a half-century of service.

Note: During this period of experimental development, classification of fighting ships varied from time to time and could be capricious and inconsistent, even in the same list. Subject to minor modifications, to show the material of the hull in every case and to be reasonably consistent, the descriptions given with the ship's name were in official use when each ship was in her prime.

USS *Mississippi* 1841-63
Wooden Paddle-Wheel Frigate

This rather ghostly photograph is of unusual historic interest, having been taken at Baton Rouge, Louisiana, just before a great ship met her end in action. Her upper rigging had been sent down, not merely in preparation for battle, but also to lighten her to get her over the bar and into the river whose name she bore.

The *Mississippi* was notable as a ship whose luck included a succession of able officers who got on together, and was therefore a happy ship: indeed, she was 'the most popular and best known of all steamers of the old time'. Her sister *Missouri*, on the other hand, was destroyed by fire during her first commission.

The *Mississippi* was launched in Philadelphia Navy Yard in 1841. She displaced 3,220 tons and was 229ft long and 40ft in beam. Two side-lever engines drove paddle-wheels—'side wheels' in American usage—28ft in diameter. With funnel lowered by a method of Perry's devising, her barque rig spread 19,000sq ft of canvas. In wartime she mounted one 10in and nineteen 8in smooth-bore shell guns and one light rifled gun.

She first made her name when bearing Perry's broad pendant as Commodore of the Gulf Squadron during the War with Mexico, 1846-7. 'The *Mississippi* is a paragon', he wrote then, and in 1852 he was glad to have her again in 'the Black Squadron' in which he negotiated, with equal diplomacy and firmness, the first major breach in Japan's isolation from the world. For convenience he transferred to a newer ship during this mission that extended into 1854, but he thought the *Mississippi* the better man-of-war.

Under Captain Melancthon Smith she was prominent in Farragut's operations on the lower Mississippi which led to the capture of New Orleans in 1862. Having poor night vision, Smith entrusted tactical handling of the ship to his young First Lieutenant, George Dewey, when engaging enemy forts at night. On 14 March 1863 she faced sterner opposition at Port Hudson, higher up. Confused by hot firing in both directions in the darkness, the river pilot directed the ship firmly on to a sandbank where, with fire threatening the magazine, she had to be abandoned, Dewey and Smith being last to leave. Flooding aft eventually lifted her bows off the shoal, and as she drifted down river, burning briskly, heat discharged her guns towards the enemy. 'She goes out magnificently, anyway!' said Dewey, just before she blew up. His account in the autobiography he wrote as Admiral of the Navy still makes stirring reading.

In the Royal Navy she was remembered as having given assistance, beyond the bounds of neutrality, to a British ship in action with the Pei-ho forts in China in 1859, which Flag Officer Josiah Tattnall USN excused with the remark 'Blood is thicker than water'. British officers subscribed to help him later, when down on his luck after having fought for the South in 1861-5.

HMS *Constance* 1846-76

Wooden Fourth Rate 50, later a Screw Frigate

HMS *Constance* was one of the last class of frigates designed by Sir William Symonds, Surveyor of the Navy from 1832 to 1848. They were slightly larger than his *Vernon* of 1832, proclaimed by his admirers to be the finest frigate in the world, and like her were 50-gun fourth rates. The *Constance* was the first of the four to be launched at Pembroke, where she took the water in March 1846. She was 180ft long, 52ft 9in in breadth and 2,132 tons BOM. Her figurehead portrayed the daughter of Sir James Graham, who as First Lord had selected Symonds for Surveyor. The National Maritime Museum has a splendid model made for one of Graham's successors.

Captain Sir Baldwin Walker commissioned her in April 1846 and after sailing trials with the *Raleigh*, launched a year earlier to Mr Fincham's design, she went out to the Pacific station.

Under Walker's relief, Captain G. W. C. Courtenay, she became the first of Her Majesty's major ships to enter Esquimalt harbour near Victoria, Vancouver Island. This later became the Canadian base of the Royal Navy's Pacific squadron and her name was given to the usual man-of-war anchorage, Constance Cove.

On her return to England she remained in reserve at Devonport until 1860 when she and her sisters *Arethusa* and *Octavia* were selected for conversion to screw frigates. In Devonport Dockyard she was cut in half and a 72ft length inserted amidships increased her tonnage to 3,213 tons BOM. The photograph shows that the alteration did not mar her handsome lines. At Chatham she was provided with engines by Randolph and Elder, which had two sets with three cylinders each, a high-pressure cylinder between two low-pressure ones. Steam at 60lb was cut off at half-stroke and exhausted to the LP cylinders for further expansion. These were the first compound engines in the Royal Navy. Her sisters had Penn and Maudslay engines, respectively. In 1865 on a trial cruise to Madeira in company, the *Constance* proved slightly faster than the others but her engines gave much trouble, and none of the three completed more than one commission as a steamer.

After engine repairs, Captain H. T. Burgoyne VC took the *Constance* out to the North America and West Indies station, where she assisted in putting down a rebellion in Jamaica and then in discouraging Fenians who, after helping to suppress the Confederate States, had thoughts of liberating Canada from British oppression. This threat having subsided, the *Constance* returned to Devonport in 1868 and paid off into reserve. She was broken up in 1876.

USS *Powhatan 1850-87*

Wooden Paddle Wheel Frigate

By 1850 paddle wheels were giving way to the screw in most navies, except for special purposes, but the *Powhatan*, a rather larger *Mississippi*, had qualities that kept her almost continually in service for longer than any of her contemporaries (except the iron-screw steamer *Michigan*, which remained in fresh water on the Great Lakes). Seamen believe that if a ship looks right, she probably *is* right. Her picture shows the *Powhatan* as an uncommonly majestic side-wheeler.

Launched in the Navy Yard at Norfolk, Virginia, in February 1850, she was 3,765 tons in displacement, 254ft long, of 45ft beam and 19½ft draught. Her copper boilers had to be renewed in due course but over the years her original engines, with 10lb steam pressure, drove her wheels at 10 rpm to give a steady 10 knots. With aid from her barque rig, 14 knots was claimed. Her original armament included one 11in and fourteen 9in smooth-bore shell guns, but some rifled guns were added in wartime. She remained popular with both officers and men throughout her service.

Proceeding independently, she joined Commodore M. C. Perry's squadron for his Japanese mission at Hong Kong in 1853. In earlier days, there had been complaints about the expense of maintaining the *Mississippi*'s engines; now they were favourably compared to the *Powhatan*'s. It would seem that these engines took time to get run in, for we hear nothing but good about the *Powhatan*'s engines in later life.

During the Civil War, after somewhat routine duties in the West Indies protecting trade, with a captain reputed (by Dewey) to be 'more disagreeable in more different ways than any man who ever wore naval uniform', the *Powhatan* joined the assault on Fort Fisher, guarding Wilmington, the last Atlantic port held by the Confederacy at the end of 1864.

In 1857 she survived one of the worst hurricanes in Atlantic history, during which reliable witnesses reported that she was dipping her fore yards in the sea. Despite this and other hazards, she remained operational, last of the great side-wheelers, until 1887 when she was surveyed, condemned and sold.

HMS *Duke of Wellington* 1852-1904
Wooden Screw Ship of the Line

In 1849 HMS *Windsor Castle*, a 120-gun first rate, was laid down in Pembroke Dockyard where, wrote Sir Thomas Pasley, Captain Superintendent, 'We are going on as usual, building ships as slowly as possible to keep our men employed'; since shipwrights once discharged were irrecoverable. By 1852 there was greater urgency and the yard was ordered to lengthen the ship for engines and the screw. She was cut in the middle, the after part eased down the slip, and a 15ft section inserted. A further slight addition aft made her the longest three-decker in the world. She was launched by Lady Pasley on 14 September 1852 and Mr Abethell, Master Shipwright, was given a gratuity of £75 for his skilful adaptation. The Duke of Wellington died that day and Queen Victoria promptly ordered the ship to be renamed in his memory.

Her new length of 240ft allowed her to be pierced for 142 broadside guns and she actually mounted 131. Her beam was 60ft and her displacement 6,071 tons. Napier geared engines of 700nhp gave her a speed of 10 knots on trials.

In the Russian War of 1854–6 she was flagship of the veteran Vice-Admiral Sir Charles Napier

in the Baltic in 1854. Most of the British fleet were steamers; most of our French allies' were not. Since the weaker Russians prudently refused battle and Napier had few ships well adapted to coastal operations, spectacular success was hardly to be expected, even if he had been younger.

After paying off in 1857 she became a guardship at Portsmouth and had no more sea service. The big screw three-deckers approached the limit of loading for wooden ships and were rapidly overtaken by progress. In 1869 the *Duke of Wellington* became flagship of the Commander-in-Chief, Portsmouth. The photograph shows her during this period, with the Admiral's flag at the main and carrying only 23 guns, for saluting. A fine bust of the Iron Duke as figurehead shares the vigil of the Royal Marine sentry on the forecastle above. Behind the ship's noble façade were less pleasing things: though service in her small permanent complement was popular, over-crowding and severe discomforts sometimes made it hard to preserve discipline or even decency amongst the transient majority.

In 1891 the *Victory* became flagship and the *Duke of Wellington* served as her tender until sold in 1904. It now seems remarkable that the Navy continued to live in hulks for nearly half a century after convicts had vacated them.

HMS *Agamemnon 1852-70*
Wooden Screw Second Rate Ship of the Line

John Edye, Assistant Surveyor of the Navy, designed HMS *Agamemnon* as a 91-gun second rate and the first of HM ships of the line to be laid down as a screw ship. Launched by Woolwich Dockyard in May 1852, she displaced 5,157 tons, and was 230ft long with a maximum breadth of 55½ft. She was engined by Penn with horizontal trunk engines of 600nhp which gave her a speed of 11 knots on trials, never achieved later.

Commissioned in 1853 for the Western Squadron she went to the Mediterranean when war with Russia was imminent. During the first year of the Crimean War she wore the flag of Rear-Admiral Sir Edmund Lyons, second-in-command of a fleet in the Black Sea that included only one other steam ship of the line. Neither our French allies or Russian enemies were better equipped, and the latter were even more reluctant to come out than their Baltic fleet. The *Agamemnon* was therefore confined to blockading until 17 October 1854, when she took part in a joint bombardment of the forts at Sebastopol. As a demonstration in aid of the armies besieging the city it was a somewhat expensive exercise, but it was not the disaster sometimes pictured by imaginative historians. Though his flagship was engaged and repeatedly hit at close range, Lyons refused to withdraw prematurely. Two fires were easily extinguished and the *Agamemnon*'s casualty list did not exceed four killed and 25 wounded. In 1855 Lyons was Commander-in-Chief and the *Agamemnon*, as a private ship commanded by Sir Thomas Pasley (with 'the best cook in the fleet', according to his friend Captain Harry Keppel) took part in operations in the Sea of Azov. These included the bombardment of Kinburn, where French armoured floating batteries were successfully tested, and by cutting off supplies contributed towards the fall of Sebastopol.

The photograph shows the ship at Woolwich in 1857 preparing for a novel operation—laying the Atlantic telegraph cable promoted mainly by the American capitalist Cyrus Field. The cable was shared between the *Agamemnon* and the United States screw frigate *Niagara*. Unhappily it parted with only 335 miles laid. Next year another approach was made. At a rendezvous in mid-Atlantic in July 1858 the two ships spliced their sections of cable together, and the *Niagara* laid the western section to Newfoundland and the *Agamemnon* the eastern half to Valentia in Ireland. By 6 August both ends were landed and communication was established. In October, however, the insulation failed and Field's faith was not rewarded by lasting success until 1866. By that time new construction had outmoded the *Agamemnon* and she remained in reserve at Portsmouth till her sale to shipbreakers in 1870.

HMS *Phoebe* 1854-75

Wooden Screw Frigate (converted)

HMS *Nankin*, launched in 1850, was the last British fourth rate to remain a sailing ship all her life. The *Phoebe* of 1854 and the *Sutlej* a year later were converted to screw ships in 1859–60. War with Russia had faced the Navy with a manning problem, since impressment had been abandoned without waiting to build up a body of long-service men and adequate reserves. Shortage of men left some ships—and officers—unemployed, and the brand-new *Phoebe* remained in reserve in Devonport, where she was built, until taken in hand for conversion.

This increased her length to 240½ft and her displacement to 3,584 tons. Her two-cylinder horizontal direct-acting Napier engines with a nominal 500hp drove her at nearly 11 knots at full load. Pierced for 50 broadside guns, she was now armed with 35 of greater weight. She retained her full ship rig with a sail area of 25,750sq ft.

Commissioned by Captain T. D. A. Fortescue for the Mediterranean in 1862, she came in for the end of Sir William Fanshawe Martin's command there, during which he did much to put naval discipline on a sounder and more uniform basis. His flagship, the screw three-decker *Marlborough*, made a name for smartness and efficiency that endured well into the present century.

On her return to Devonport in 1866 the *Phoebe* was refitted and in May 1867 recommissioned by Captain John Bythesea VC for the North America and West Indies station. Two years later she was diverted to 'Particular Service', which in her case meant joining the Flying Squadron, four frigates and two corvettes under Rear-Admiral Geoffrey Phipps Hornby, another outstanding admiral, on a training cruise round the world. The First Lord, Mr Childers, used this to justify reducing the ships on foreign stations: *The Times* predicted that he would be remembered as 'Flying' Childers, but his example was later followed by Lord Fisher.

The *Phoebe* joined at Bahia, replacing the *Bristol*, and was inspected at sea on the way to the Cape. The routine was strenuous and steam was raised only when necessary: Hornby's orders should be studied by those who believe that Fisher was unique in enforcing economy. The cruise included Australia, New Zealand, Japan, Esquimalt (where *The British Colonist* described the squadron as 'the grandest sight the Pacific has ever known'), Honolulu, Valparaiso and the Falklands, arriving at Plymouth on 15 November 1870. The cruise was considered a great success despite the loss of some men, mainly to the Australian goldfields. This was the *Phoebe*'s last seagoing service, and she was sold in 1875.

HMS *Magnet 1856-74*

Wooden 'Crimean' Screw Gunboat

It has already been mentioned that in the Russian War of 1854–6 the absence of enemy opposition at sea confined allied naval operations to blockade and attack on the enemy coasts, and that there was a shortage of vessels with the necessary armament and shallow draught for the latter purpose. HMS *Magnet* was one of a host of gunboats mainly ordered from private shipbuilders to fill this gap. She was launched by Briggs at Sunderland in January 1856. There were 118 sisters in the *Dapper* class to which she belonged, and some 38 rather lighter types.

The designed dimensions of the *Dappers* were: 233 tons burthen, 106ft length, 22ft beam, 6⅔ft draught. Their horizontal engines of 60nhp developed nearly 200ihp at a pressure of about 35lb, giving a speed of 7½ knots, sometimes. Their standard rig was fore-and-aft as the photograph indicates. Their armament varied, but in 1856 commonly included one 68 and one 32-pounder and two 12-pounder brass howitzers. (In this context a howitzer was a light gun for firing shells at elevations from the horizontal to about 12°.)

Despite their comic appearance they had great virtues. One distinguished admiral remembered them as 'the handiest vessels I ever knew' and another as 'wonderfully well constructed'. In their heyday in 1856 the young lieutenants working up their first commands created interest, amusement and havoc on the South Coast. 'They neither knows nothin' nor fears nothin' ' said the Portsmouth longshoremen. The Port Admiral reckoned they cost the taxpayer £85 a week in repairs—a substantial sum in those uninflated days.

Twenty of the class served in the Baltic or the Black Sea in 1855, but for some their first and last appearance was made at the Royal Review held at Spithead on St. George's Day 1856, to mark the end of the war. Sixteen saw active service in China, four went to the Mediterranean, three were seen in Bermuda and Halifax and the *Forward* and *Grappler* served usefully in British

Columbian waters for several years in the 1860s.

The *Magnet* was for some time a tender to HMS *Pembroke*, guardship at Harwich, and then went into reserve at Sheerness. When she was broken up at Chatham in 1874 she was outlived by about 16 sisters. The short life of some was mainly due to being built of unseasoned wood, unavoidable in an emergency programme at this time.

HMS *Sparrowhawk 1856-72*
Wooden Screw Gun Vessel

HMS *Sparrowhawk* belonged to a class of fourteen ships ordered in 1855 for the Russian War. Originally 'Despatch Vessels', they were also referred to as 'Gun Vessels' and 'Sloops', but firmly became Gun Vessels under an Admiralty Order in 1862 defining these as 'Vessels commanded by Commanders and carrying their principal armament on one deck amidships'. This meant that their big guns were secured on the centre line but could be traversed to fire on either side. They were designed by the Surveyor's Department (Chief Constructor, Isaac Watts) and built by contract with private firms on the Thames and at Cowes, the *Sparrowhawk* by Young and Magnay of Limehouse.

Some latitude seems to have been allowed, since the National Maritime Museum's records suggest that the twin funnels and knee bow shown in the photograph, taken at Esquimalt, British Columbia, were not common to the whole class. She was 676 tons BOM (860 tons displacement), $180\frac{2}{3}$ft long and $28\frac{1}{2}$ft in breadth. Engined by Humphrys and Tennant with two-cylinder horizontal engines and 3 boilers working at 20lb she achieved $10\frac{1}{2}$ knots on trials. She had a lifting screw and was barque rigged, without royals. From 1865 her armament included one 7in gun, one 68-pounder, and two 20-pounders. The latter and the 7in were breech-loading.

After attending the Spithead Review on St George's Day 1856 she was paid off but was recommissioned in 1857 for the East Indies and China station where she served until 1861 and took part in the Second China War. On return she went into reserve at Portsmouth until March 1865, when Commander E. A. Porcher commissioned her for the Pacific. There she was employed mainly on the coast of British Columbia, where her name is recalled by Sparrowhawk Rock near Port Simpson. She was sometimes used as a yacht or despatch vessel by the Commander-in-Chief. In 1868 she was recommissioned on the station by Commander H. W. Mist. In July 1871 after British Columbia became part of Canada, she conveyed ex-Governor Musgrave to San Francisco and brought back his successor, with reduced status. Soon after, the *Sparrowhawk* was ordered home but she had now outlived all her sisters, and on reconsideration she was sold on the station in 1872. Her engines were removed to a mill at Moodyville and lasted until 1909. The ship made two or three voyages to China with timber but was lost in a typhoon.

USS *Brooklyn 1858-91*

Wooden Screw Sloop

Dressed with flags overall, yards manned, and firing a salute from bow guns, the *Brooklyn* is seen here at a naval review on 29 April 1889, near the end of thirty years' service. The men on the yards are steadied by a jackstay at waist level behind them. In the Royal Navy, they would

stand closer together with an overlapping grip on the jackstay, their arms crossing at the wrist. These men appear to have cap in hand, perhaps preparing to cheer. Manning the bowsprit and jib-boom seems to be an American innovation.

Built and engined by Jacob Westervelt of New York, the *Brooklyn* displaced nearly 3,000 tons and was 233ft long, 43ft in beam. She had a two-cylinder simple engine with jet condenser, giving 1,165ihp and a speed of 10 to 11 knots. She had a two-bladed hoisting propeller, a telescopic funnel (seen nearly down in the photograph), and was ship rigged. Her original armament comprised one 10in and twenty 9in smooth-bore guns, 'spoken of distinctively as shell guns' (says Captain Mahan) 'because not expected to fire solid shot under ordinary circumstances'.

First commissioned on 26 January 1859 by Captain David Glasgow Farragut, she served in the West Indies and Gulf of Mexico and had worked up to full efficiency before the Civil War, during which it was acknowledged that no ships gave better service than her class. Between 1861 and 1864 she was in the West Gulf Blockading Squadron under Farragut's command, and helped capture New Orleans in 1862, but was absent when the *Mississippi* was lost next year. On 5 August 1864, having better ahead fire than the others, she was selected to lead the squadron into Mobile Bay. Under instructions from Farragut to keep inside a buoy believed to mark a line of mines (then called 'torpedoes'), she found herself being headed off by friendly monitors into what seemed to be 'torpedo' buoys to port of her. She stopped and was swung across the fairway, raked by fire from Fort Morgan, and might have doomed the whole assault, but for the bold action taken by Farragut, to be described later. Captain Alden of the *Brooklyn* came in for some harsh and not entirely fair criticism, but earned praise for his handling of the ship during the operation against Fort Fisher at the turn of the year.

After the War, the *Brooklyn* had a world-wide range of nearly continuous service, ending with the Asiatic Squadron in 1886–9, returning just in time for this review. After it, she was finally de-commissioned at New York on 14 May 1889 and was sold in March 1891.

USS *Hartford* 1858-1956
Wooden Screw Sloop

The *Hartford*, similar to the *Brooklyn*, was the most famous and longest-lived of that group of five ships completed just in time to give invaluable service in the Civil War. Built in the Boston Navy Yard, she was launched in 1858 with three sponsors sprinkling different brands of water over her bows—an unusual 'triple-barreled water ceremony' but at least it brought her no ill-luck. Her dimensions were slightly less than the *Brooklyn*'s and her original armament was twenty-two 9in shell guns, but was otherwise like her, though Captain Mahan allows her only 8 knots. She had the same full ship rig typical of the first stages of the transition from sail to steam.

Recalled from the Far East, she became in 1862 the flagship of Farragut's West Gulf Blockading Squadron, with orders to capture New Orleans. Sixty-one years old, with only seven years' service as a captain, and in his first command of a squadron, Farragut proved himself the outstanding naval commander of the war. By a combination of thorough preparation and resolute dash, he forced his way past all defences and received the surrender of New Orleans.

On 16 July 1862 he became the first Rear-Admiral in the United States Navy. Previously it was felt that 'admiral' had 'a royal and authoritative flavour' and captain had been the highest

American rank. When commanding a squadron, a captain received the courtesy title of 'Commodore' or, since 1857, 'Flag Officer'.

After tightening the coastal blockade, Farragut returned up the Mississippi in 1863 to assist the army besieging Vicksburg. Before passing the defences of Port Hudson, he laid down as a maxim: 'The best protection against the enemy's fire is a well-directed fire from our own guns'; but he did not neglect other steps. In the event, advancing with three pairs of ships and the *Mississippi*, two pairs were crippled and the *Mississippi* lost, but the *Hartford* and *Albatross* got through and helped to isolate Vickburg, which surrendered in July.

In August 1864 the operations against Mobile, where the Confederates were improvising ironclads in the hope of breaking the blockade, finally established Farragut's claim to greatness. His golden moment came when the *Brooklyn*'s dilemma threatened to throw the whole force into disarray. Though the risk was shown by the monitor *Tecumseh* foundering in the minefield, Farragut paused only a moment before deciding: 'Damn the torpedoes! Captain Draycott, go ahead!' He got the luck he deserved. Though 'torpedoes' were heard scraping the hull, and several ships were later sunk in the area, no more exploded at this time and complete victory followed. In fairness to Captain Alden, we may note that Farragut was in a better position to ignore his own cautionary instructions, and even he sought divine guidance before doing so.

Ill-health obliged Farragut to give up command and towards the end of the year the *Hartford* returned him to a hero's welcome in New York, with promotion to Vice-Admiral. The *Hartford* continued to be a seagoing flagship until 1884, when she was used for training and as a station ship until 1926. In 1945 she was towed to Norfolk Navy Yard. Classified as a relic, she lay there until November 1956, when she sank at her moorings and was dismantled, just short of her century.

HMS *Charybdis 1859-84*

Wooden Screw Corvette

'Corvette', borrowed from the French early in the century, was at first a term more readily accepted colloquially than officially by the Royal Navy, but had reached the Navy List before the Pearl class, including the *Charybdis*, were on the slip. At this time it meant a ship just below the frigate, but large enough to be a captain's command, usually carrying her armament on the upper deck.

Designed by Isaac Watts primarily for foreign service, this class had full ship rig with auxiliary engines and a hoisting propeller. The *Charybdis*, built in Chatham Dockyard, had Miller, Ravenhill and Salkeld's two-cylinder horizontal engines of 1,400ihp, supplied with steam at 20lb giving a trial speed of 10 knots. She originally had twenty 8in guns on truck carriages and one 68-pounder on a pivot mounting as a chase gun forward. 200ft long and displacing 2,187 tons, she was larger and much more formidable than the 6th rates scornfully called 'jackass frigates' fifty years before, but she did not escape a revival of this unfair derision.

All her service was abroad. On both her first and second commissions she fetched up in the Pacific on the west coast of North America, after starting on the China and Australian stations, respectively. After a mishap on that coast, she was repaired in time to join Hornby's Flying Squadron for passage to Honolulu and Valparaiso but returned to British Columbia until 1871.

From 1873 to 1880 she was on the China station, recommissioning there, although maintenance facilities were modest. When she returned to England late in 1880 she was handed over to an agent of the Canadian Government to provide a training ship as a first step towards a local naval force. By the time she arrived at St John after a six weeks' passage, her age and inadequate maintenance were all too evident. Considered beyond economical repair, she was taken to Halifax and formally returned to Vice-Admiral Sir Leopold M'Clintock, the Commander-in-Chief, who had her sold locally for £2,150. As an aid to encouraging a new 'colonial' Navy, the gift of the *Charybdis* was even more shortsighted than the sale of the obsolescent *Niobe* and *Rainbow* to Canada in 1910.

HMS *Warrior 1860- (still afloat)*
Armour-plated Iron Screw Ship

'Two wonderful ships, totally different in almost every principle from every ship yet launched in the history of the world.' This was said of the *Warrior* and her sister *Black Prince* by Lord Hampton who, as Sir John Pakington, First Lord of the Admiralty, had approved their construction in answer to the *Gloire* launched by France in 1859.

As late as 1849 iron was condemned, not only by the Admiralty but by the French and American navies as well, as unsuitable for major war vessels because of the fragmentation and jagged holes produced by shot and shell. Since then iron had improved in quality, developments in ordnance demanded better protection, and French armoured batteries had shown in the Russian War that it could be provided. In the *Gloire*, France's great naval architect, Dupuy de Lôme, encased the wooden hull of a second rate in stout armour. Isaac Watts, advised by Scott Russell, an enterprising private shipbuilder, designed the *Warrior* as an iron ship with iron frames. Steam three-deckers were approaching or exceeding the length permitted by wooden construction, and were racked by both the weight and the vibration of their machinery. The *Warrior* was 120ft longer and displaced one-third more than any first-rate. Watertight bulkheads gave her new internal safety

impossible in an oak hull that 'worked' under stress in a seaway. A 4½in armour belt, backed by 18in of teak, extended the length of her powerful battery and was closed at the ends.

Built at Blackwall by Ditchburn and Mare, she displaced 9,210 tons on a length of 380ft and a beam of 58¼ft. Penn's horizontal trunk engines developing over 5,000ihp gave her a speed of 14.3 knots on trials. Ten rectangular boilers provided steam at 20lb. Her original armament included twenty-six 68-pounders and fourteen breech-loading guns of Armstrong's new design. A full ship rig was needed to give her adequate strategic mobility and she achieved up to 13 knots under canvas. Her weakest features were her unarmoured ends and the unsupported weight of her knee bow and frigate stern, which were expensive concessions to appearance.

Her photograph shows her at Plymouth during her first commission in the Channel Squadron in 1861–4 (the date is confirmed by the Red Ensign at her stern, for the Red and Blue squadronal ensigns based on the grade of the flag officer in command were abolished in 1864). Most of her seagoing was in home waters and she saw no active service, but effectively helped to keep European peace for a quarter of a century. From 1904 she formed part of HMS *Vernon*, the torpedo school at Portsmouth, until it moved ashore in 1923. Since then she has supported an oil pipeline at Pembroke. The Maritime Trust, which has been successful in saving a number of other historic vessels, has her preservation in view when she ceases her present useful role. As Admiral Ballard emphasised, though the *Warrior* lacks the *Victory*'s historical laurels, as a technical advance she was in a class of her own.

USS *Kearsarge* 1861-94
Wooden Screw Sloop

The *Kearsarge*, sometimes called a corvette, belonged to the *Mohican* class of sloops, designed about the same time as the *Brooklyn*, but on smaller lines, and barque-rigged, as can be seen in the photograph taken in New York harbour about 1890.

Built in Portsmouth, New Hampshire, Navy Yard (geographically located a little up-river in Kittery, Maine), she displaced 1,550 tons on a length of 201ft, 14ft beam, and a mean draught of 14ft 6in. She was armed with two 11in Dahlgren shell guns, four 32-pounder smooth-bores and one 30-pounder rifled gun. Her engines developed 822ihp, giving her a maximum speed of 11 knots; 9 knots was perhaps more realistic on service.

Launched 11 September 1861, with wartime haste she was commissioned on 24 January 1862 and sailed on 5 February to hunt the Confederate commerce raider *Sumter*, commanded by Captain Raphael Semmes CSN, which had eluded the *Brooklyn* at the mouth of the Mississippi some months earlier. Closely blockaded in Gibraltar, Semmes abandoned the *Sumter*, but in July took over a new raider, smuggled out of the Mersey under false papers, and renamed her *Alabama*. In nearly two years of cruising she captured sixty-nine Union merchant ships.

In June 1864, news of her arrival at Cherbourg reached the *Kearsarge*, then off Holland and commanded by Captain John Winslow, a former friend and cabin-mate of Semmes. On arrival off Cherbourg, he received a challenge from Semmes who took the *Alabama* out on the 19th, escorted clear of territorial waters by a French warship. The two opponents closed to engage on opposite courses, starboard broadside to starboard broadside, and continued to circle, preserving their relative positions though carried along on the tide. The *Kearsarge* had an advantage in guns, gunners and powder that decided the contest two hours, and seven circles, later when the *Alabama* struck her colours, just before foundering. Semmes and 40 of his crew were saved by the

Deerhound, an English yacht watching the action.

The subsequent war service of the *Kearsarge* included hunts for two more Confederate raiders which were otherwise disposed of. In the following thirty years, apart from refitting interludes, she was employed on practically every station on a variety of duties, including taking a scientific party to Vladivostock to observe a transit of Venus. On 2 February 1894 on passage from Haiti to Bluefields, in Nicaragua, she grounded on Roncador Reef. $45,000 was appropriated for salvage, but without success, and she had to be removed from the Register of the Navy.

USS *Franklin* 1864–1915

Wooden Screw Frigate

As an example of the expedients to which the United States Navy was sometimes forced during periods of retrenchment, this *Franklin*—here shown about 1885 when she had become a receiving ship at Norfolk, Virginia—deserves a high place. Since Congress in the early 1850s was unwilling to provide funds for new ships, the Navy's Bureau of Construction and Repair, disrespectfully known as the 'Bureau of Destruction and Despair', decided to 're-build' the *Franklin*, launched in 1814 as a 74-gun sailing ship-of-the-line, into a new screw frigate nearly half as large again. It is said some of the old wood went into the new hull.

The old *Franklin* was taken to pieces at Portsmouth Navy Yard in 1853 and the new one laid

down in 1854. Funds were so limited, however, that it was ten years before she was launched on 17 September 1864, and a contract was placed for her machinery. She displaced 5,170 tons and was 265ft long, and 54ft in beam. The disposition of her armament made her nominally a frigate, but its weight and power—one 11in and thirty-nine 9in SB shell guns and four 100-pounder rifles—plus the mobility given by her engines made her more formidable than any sailing first rate. On the other hand, she was not in the same league with the ironclads Britain and France were building at this time.

On 3 June 1867, Captain Pennock commissioned her at Boston to become the flagship of the US European Squadron, re-established after the war. On 25 July 1866, Congress had created the rank of Admiral in the United States Navy and bestowed it upon Farragut. He hoisted his four-star flag on 17 June 1867 and was given permission to embark his wife and a companion for an extended tour of the main sea ports of Europe. An American historian suggests that 'he must have been embarrassed to receive dignitaries aboard his wooden flagship' but it is hard to imagine a man of his calibre being seriously disturbed by what then might seem a passing symptom of a period of reconstruction. During 1868 his tour was extended to include Minorca whence his father had emigrated to America in 1776, and to Malta and Constantinople. He returned to New York on 10 November, after what had been throughout a triumphal progress. Less than two years later he died at Norfolk, one of those rare characters whom it is hard to fault.

The ship completed two further commissions as a flagship before being paid off at Norfolk on 2 March 1877, recommissioning next day as receiving ship for that station. In this capacity of a depot ship she remained until October 1915, when she was struck from the Navy List and sold.

HMS *Agincourt 1865-1960*
Armour-plated Iron Screw Ship
(A coal hulk from 1909)

The *Agincourt* and her sister *Minotaur* with their half-sister *Northumberland* were the last and largest battleships designed by Watts. After the *Warrior* he had been curbed by economy but in these three ships he had generous scope for armament, protection and speed.

Launched by Laird at Birkenhead in March 1865, the *Agincourt* was 400ft long with a beam of 59½ft and 10,690 tons displacement. Ten rectangular boilers supplied steam at 25lb pressure to two-cylinder Maudslay return connecting-rod engines, which on trials developed 6,870ihp and a speed of 14.8 knots. Her single screw could be disconnected when sailing, but though her array of canvas looked impressive it was said that 'No ships ever carried so much dress to so little purpose' and the screw was needed to manage her, particularly in company. Her armament consisted of twenty-four 7in and four 9in muzzle-loading rifled guns, Armstrong's breech-loaders being under suspicion. An armour belt of 5½in maximum thickness covered all the waterline and protected the battery.

For most of twenty years the *Minotaur* and *Agincourt* were flagships of the Channel Squadron. The *Minotaur* was normally senior but had fewer changes of flag and a remarkably uneventful career. The *Agincourt* with the *Northumberland* towed a floating dock for Bermuda to Madeira in 1868, and in 1869 had the exceptional privilege of hoisting the Admiralty flag while the Board headed by the First Lord, Mr Hugh Childers, took charge of a combined fleet, very little to anyone's satisfaction. Two years later leaving Gibraltar in 1871, heading the lee line in station abeam of the *Minotaur*, she impaled herself upon the Pearl Rock and was lucky to be towed off three days later. This provided a *cause célèbre*, on which the Admiralty reasonably considered that blame was not entirely confined to the *Agincourt*. In 1873 while the *Minotaur* was rearming she flew the Commander-in-Chief's flag; and four years later, as second flagship in the Mediterranean for a change, she accompanied Admiral Hornby through the Dardanelles in

a blinding snowstorm to check a Russian move on Constantinople. She was second flagship at the Queen's Golden Jubilee Review in 1887 and took part in the manoeuvres afterward. Two years later she was relegated to a training role, but she appeared under sail at the Diamond Jubilee Review with her boys under training.

In 1909 she sank to a coal-hulk at Sheerness, remaining as C109 until scrapped in 1960, nearly a century after she was laid down.

USS *Florida, ex-Wampanoag, 1868-85*

Wooden Screw Cruiser, or Sloop

This photograph shows the *Florida* in dock in the New York Navy Yard (sited in Brooklyn, Long Island) in 1874, with a lot of timber and a limber for shifting it in the foreground. The ship's remarkable appearance, meant to be alarming, is matched by her short and contentious history. Late in the Civil War, the US Navy laid down half a dozen fast cruisers primarily to discourage British or French intervention in the war, with hunting Confederate raiders as an alternative—ie, to act as poacher or gamekeeper, as the situation required. With Gettysburg won and the Mississippi open, however, risk of intervention disappeared, and at low priority the ships did not reach trials until 1868.

The most promising was the *Wampanoag*, designed by Naval Constructor B. F. Delano, built in the NY Navy Yard and, appropriately, engined by the Novelty Iron Works to the designs of Benjamin Isherwood, head of the Bureau of Steam Engineering. She displaced 4,215 tons and was 335ft long. Her engines had a pair of cylinders 100in in diameter and a 4ft stroke. Huge wooden gear wheels drove the propeller at 2 revolutions for each double piston stroke. She had a surface condenser and eight vertical tubular boilers, with four superheaters.

As designed, she was barque rigged (subsequently reduced to fore and aft sails, as the photograph shows), and her first trial was under sail. Under steam, she worked up to speed and maintained

17 knots or thereabouts for 38 hours. Her Captain, J. W. A. Nicholson, stated in writing his opinion that the ship was 'faultless in her model, and as a steamship the fastest in the world'; and a board of three Chief Engineers, USN, considered that she was not equalled 'for speed and economy by any seagoing screw vessel in the world'.

On the other hand, a board under Rear-Admiral Goldsborough decided, overriding two dissentient engineers, that it was 'utterly impracticable to make her a vessel of war worthy of our navy' and recommended reducing her power and giving her a ship rig with more canvas.

Bennett, in *The Steam Navy of the United States*, as an engineer himself, is indignant at the failure to exploit an advance in speed which the British—'more progressive and less hide-bound in these matters than ourselves'—did not reach for another ten years.

Be that as it may, the *Florida*, as she was renamed in 1869, was left in reserve in Brooklyn until 1874, when she was sent to New London, Connecticut, as a receiving and store ship. The white oak of which these ships were built was shortlived, and in 1885 she was sold for $41,508—about 3 per cent of her cost, but that is taking a commercial view of a considerable engineering stride.

HMS *Captain* 1869-70
Armoured Iron Turret Ship

HMS *Captain*'s brief life was fraught with controversy that continued after her loss. She was the conception of Captain Cowper Coles RN who saw that the problems arising from the increasing size and weight of guns might best be met by mounting them in turrets on the weather deck. Like Ericsson who was independently pursuing this line in America, he advocated a well-protected hull with a low freeboard: unlike Ericsson, he included a full rig in his seagoing version. Rejecting the doubts of the Admiralty's technical advisers and their notions of a turret ship—embodied in the 'masted' *Monarch* with normal freeboard and limited arcs of fire, and in the *Devastation*, without sails—he conducted a publicity campaign that gained support from the public, press and First Lord. The Controller, Admiral Sir Spencer Robinson, and Reed, Watts' successor as Chief Constructor, declined responsibility but under duress accepted a thoroughly British compromise, namely, entrusting a reputable private contractor to develop Coles's ideas.

Lairds of Birkenhead undertook this, but for seaworthiness had to add a forecastle and poop, limiting the turrets' arcs of training, and joined them by a flying deck. The National Maritime Museum has a model clearly showing the layout. Surprisingly, Coles did not demur. The turrets each carried two 12in 25 ton guns, and 7in guns fore and aft provided end on fire, all muzzle-loading rifles. The side was armoured to upper deck level and the turrets well protected. A length of 320ft and 54½ft beam gave a ratio of 6:1, assisting her twin screws to drive her at 14¼ knots. Her trunk engines were provided by Lairds. The photograph alongside at Portsmouth shows her ship rig and the tripod masts adopted to limit the rigging's interference with arcs of fire. Her weakness lay in her modest beam and a freeboard reduced from 8½ to 6½ft by 800 tons added to her designed displacement during building. Once her upper deck was awash her stability fell off rapidly if she continued to heel.

Robinson and Reed remained distrustful, but the new First Lord, Mr Hugh Childers, showed his faith by transferring his son to her from the *Monarch*. She made two successful trial cruises in company but each night the admiral, Sir Thomas Symonds, ordered her to have steam immediately available. By one of life's grimmer ironies, he was removed by Childers before the night of 1 September 1870 when the *Captain* capsized in a gale off the Spanish coast. The Gunner and seventeen men escaped in the pinnace; 472 drowned, including Coles himself, Captain Hugh Burgoyne VC and Midshipman Childers. Many felt that this did not entirely excuse the First Lord's violent reaction to the court-martial verdict, which implied that some blame was attributable to the Admiralty, for having built the *Captain* 'in deference to public opinion expressed in Parliament, and through other channels, and in opposition to the views and opinions of the Controller and his department', and also for not having fully ascertained and promulgated the facts about her stability.

The small print shows the view from the poop of the *Captain* looking forward along the flying deck. The foot of the port leg of the mizzen tripod is clearly visible.

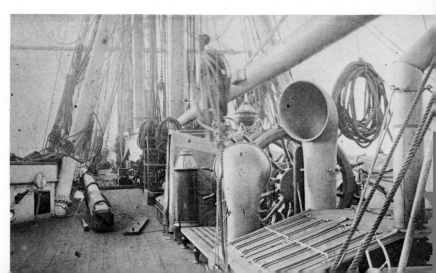

HMS *Volage 1869-1904*

Iron Screw Corvette, cased with Wood

Unarmoured men-of-war did not match the remarkable, if still experimental, progress of capital ships in the 1860s. Economy and the emphasis on coastal operations in the Russian and Chinese wars were partly responsible. In addition, suspicion cast by gun trials of the 1840s upon iron hulls without armour delayed their adoption. Wooden ships, however, could not carry high-powered engines without strain, so screw frigates and corvettes lacked the steaming speed demanded by their functions—until reports of fast American frigates and the known speed achieved by merchantmen eventually impelled the Admiralty to lay down iron-hulled cruising types.

HMS *Volage* and her sister the *Active* were both launched at Blackwall by the Thames Shipbuilding Company in 1869. Though classed as corvettes, they had the necessary qualities to play the cruiser role of the old fifth-rates. Displacing 3,080 tons, with a length of 270ft and beam of 42ft, the *Volage* had Penn trunk engines and five rectangular boilers giving steam at 30lb pressure, which produced 4,532ihp and a trial speed of 15 knots. A graceful knee bow was balanced by a sloping stern with painted ports. She was originally armed with six 7in and two 6in rifled muzzle-loaders on the upper deck and one of the latter on topgallant forecastle and poop. The upper deck armament was later replaced by ten 6in BL guns. Under sail she was handy, with a best speed of about 13 knots. She and the *Active*, with the large new frigate *Inconstant*, were then the only cruisers that could steam faster than they sailed.

The *Volage* did an exceptional amount of sailing during her long career, which included service with the Flying Squadron in 1871–2. Sail training was still highly esteemed and the *Volage* passed five commissions with a Training Squadron under sail. In 1894 she and the *Active*, wearing the Commodore's broad pendant, were the last ships to leave Portsmouth unaided by steam. The squadron paid off in 1899 when it seemed to offer an unnecessary hostage to fortune at a period of strained relations. The *Volage* was sold in 1904.

HMS *Vulture 1869-85*

Wooden Twin-Screw Gun Vessel

HMS *Vulture* was the eleventh of a class of gun vessels launched in royal yards between 1867 and 1869; the *Woodlark*, twelfth and last of class, followed in 1871. The gun vessel was still defined in the Navy List as a ship commanded by a Commander and carrying her main armament on one deck amidships. Here we see behind his whiskers the Commander, Robert Cay, with his First Lieutenant and a mixed group of officers and ratings including a fiddler. Before them is a 7in MLR gun secured on the centreline, with the rollers on its carriage that enabled it to be traversed to fire on either side.

Because coastal bombardment remained very much in mind, these vessels were given twin screws, not as a technical advance but as a step reluctantly accepted to obtain the shallow draught needed for coastal operations. Except for iron cross-beams, the hull was wood, with a square-bilged cross-section. 170ft long, 29ft in beam, with a maximum load draught of 10½ft, they displaced 755 tons. The *Vulture*'s Rennie engines and rectangular boilers working at 30lb pressure gave her a trial speed of 10.8 knots, the fastest—or least slow—of the class. They were the smallest ships with telescopic funnels, instead of being hinged for lowering to avoid interference with sails. Rigged as barques, with pole topmasts and without royals, they sailed as well as might be expected with the drag of twin screws, but they made much leeway and needed engine power to keep them up to a wind. Their original armament consisted of the 7in gun and two Armstrong 40-pounder breech-loaders, but the latter were replaced by 64-pounder MLR guns when breech-loaders went temporarily out of favour. Accommodation was cramped and exceedingly hot in the tropics, and the *Vulture* and five others later acquired a poop and topgallant forecastle. The second photograph shows her so modified, drying her sails.

After completing in Sheerness Dockyard, the *Vulture* spent two years in reserve before being commissioned for the East Indies by Cay. In 1874, now commanded by A. T. Brooke, she took

Doctor Livingstone's body, carried 1,000 miles to the coast by his faithful African companions, from Bagamoyo to Zanzibar. Having refitted at home in 1875, she was again commissioned for the East Indies and served there from 1876 to 1880. Her name was long remembered in the Persian Gulf for her anti-slavery work, particularly for an affair near El Katif, where her armed boats broke up a concentration of piratical dhows, capturing twenty. On return to England she was placed in reserve until sold for breaking up in 1885.

HMS *Raleigh* 1873-1905

Iron Screw Frigate, sheathed with Wood
(later classified as a Cruiser 2nd Class)

HMS *Raleigh*, and the larger *Shah* launched the same year, were the last of HM ships to be designated frigates until the term was revived in World War II for a very different type.

Like the *Volage*, the *Raleigh* was iron in frame and hull, sheathed with wood and coppered, but she displaced 4,780 tons. Her length was 298ft, beam 49ft, and she drew $23\frac{1}{2}$ft. Her Humphrys and Tennant return connecting-rod engines, fed by nine boilers at 30lb pressure, and driving a hoisting propeller, gave her $15\frac{1}{2}$ knots. She was a good seaboat and a steady gun platform. Her original armament, lighter than the *Shah*'s, included twenty-two guns of three calibres, two 9in, fourteen 7in and six 6in, all muzzle-loading rifles. Most were replaced by breech-loaders later. Her ship rig was not on the maximum scale but gave her a respectable speed, especially in a fresh breeze. She brought her cable directly to a patent capstan and her figurehead, one of the last in the Royal Navy, was a half-length of Sir Walter, and her hull had decorations of the potato and tobacco leaves associated with his westward voyages.

Launched in Chatham Dockyard and commissioned by Captain George Tryon, she joined the Flying Squadron and in Indian waters was selected to escort the *Serapis* carrying HRH the Prince of Wales, the future Edward VII, home after a royal durbar in 1875. She then completed a commission in the Mediterranean, and recommissioned for a trooping voyage to Australia, east-about, doubling both Capes and becoming the last British frigate to pass Cape Horn under canvas.

A long refit and re-armament in 1881–4 increased her displacement to 5,640 tons. Between 1885 and 1895 she was for three commissions flagship on the Cape station. Sir F. C. D. Bedford was the last admiral to hoist his flag at a mizzen topgallant masthead at sea. In 1889–90 she was briefly sent as a private ship to reinforce the East Indies Squadron during a slight difficulty with Portugal, one incident of which was embellished out of all recognition in Kipling's 'Judson and the Empire'. 'Judson' is supposed to have been drawn from Lieutenant de Horsey of the *Raleigh* and Kipling certainly had her in mind in describing his fictional '*Martin Frobisher*' as 'a great war-boat when she was new, in the days when men built for sail as well as for steam'.

In 1898 she hoisted the Commodore's broad pendant in the Training Squadron, but was paid off after October 1899 when the Boer War ended sail training on that scale. She was sold in 1905.

The second photograph shows four officers of the *Raleigh* on board her about 1889. They are from left to right: Lieutenant Charles E. Madden, Torpedo Officer; P. G. V. van der Byl, First Lieutenant; and Lieutenants S. V. Y. de Horsey and Reg Gregory, two of her watchkeepers. Madden was Jellicoe's Chief of Staff in the Grand Fleet 1914–16, second in command under Beatty and in command of the 1st Battle Squadron 1916–19, promoted to Admiral of the Fleet in 1924 and served as First Sea Lord 1927–30. De Horsey became a full admiral; Gregory retired as a captain and van der Byl as a commander.

HMS *Egeria 1873–1911*

Composite Screw Sloop (later Surveying Vessel)

On 22 January 1901, after Queen Victoria's death, HMS *Egeria*, as her only ship then in Esquimalt, had the sad duty of firing her final salute—81 minute-guns, one for every year of her life, from obsolete 20-pounder BLR guns of Armstrong's original pattern. A shovel held over the vent to protect the awning was promptly blown through it. The awning was therefore triced up as in the photograph, which also shows the ensign and jack at half-mast.

With five sisters also launched in 1873–4, the *Egeria* was one of the first British composite sloops, with an iron frame and a teak shell. They displaced 940 tons, were 160ft long and $31\frac{1}{2}$ft in breadth, and drew 14ft aft. They were armed with two 7in $4\frac{1}{2}$ ton and two 64-pounder MLR traversing guns. Despite being the first sloops to have compound (double expansion) engines, both their maximum speed and steaming radius were modest, being about 11 knots and 1,000 miles at 10 knots respectively. All their service was on foreign stations, where they depended heavily upon their barque rig. (The mizzen yards in the photograph were clearly crossed only for appearance sake—not an uncommon practice.) Four of the class besides the *Egeria* served in the Pacific.

She went out to China in 1874, survived a grounding off Hainan after re-commissioning locally in 1878, and came home in 1881. Presently she was converted for surveying, receiving a poop and extra boats, and exchanging her guns for Armstrong's, considered adequate to deal

with pirates. Sailing in 1886 she completed another two commissions abroad, surveying in Chinese, Malayan and Australian waters and sounding in great depths for an Australian—BC telegraph cable. In 1894 she was re-boilered and refitted and in 1897 went out to the Pacific for a long spell of strenuous surveying, mainly in British Columbian waters around Vancouver Island, but including a passage to Honolulu doing further sounding for the trans-Pacific cable, determining the longitude of Vancouver and Esquimalt westward of McGill University, (using the CPR telegraph), and in 1907 surveying the Gardner Canal as a possible terminal for the Grand Trunk Pacific. Her captains included two future Surveyors of the Navy, Admirals Parry and Learmonth. In 1910 she completed the major task started twelve years earlier and she was sold next year in Vancouver. There she served the Boys' Naval Brigade until 1914, when the Kaiser's War finished her, with much else.

USS *Vandalia* 1874-89

Wooden Screw Corvette

(Screw Steamer, 3rd Rate, according to Chief Engr King)

The large photograph is taken from the poop of the *Vandalia*, looking forward. Drawn up athwartships is her guard, provided by the United States Marine Corps, whose Hymn, it may be recalled, begins:

'From the Halls of Montezuma to the shores of Tripoli
We fight our country's battles, on the land as on the sea'

and concludes:

      'If the Army or the Navy ever look on Heaven's scenes
      They will find the streets are guarded by United States Marines.'

On either side are three 9in smooth-bore muzzle-loading guns, firing through ports in the bulwarks. These are topped by hammock-rails in which the men's bedding is stowed under canvas covers. The telescopic funnel, before the mainmast, is in a lowered position. Beyond it, again, a light bridge spans the bulwarks.

The *Vandalia*, nominally a re-build of a sailing sloop of 1828, was launched in Boston Navy Yard in 1874. Her displacement was 2,100 tons, length 216ft and beam 39ft. Her engines developed 1,176ihp on trials and gave her a maximum speed of 12 knots. Besides the six 9in guns shown she carried an 8in breech-loading rifled gun which could be fired on either side, and a lighter 60-pounder BL gun as a chase gun on the forecastle.

Within the limits allowed by strict economy, she was a fine ship, and in 1878, returning after three years abroad, could claim to have steamed 26,280 miles and never been detained a day for repairs. 'Such a record can rarely be found in a United States Navy log', says *The Steam Navy of the United States*. It must then have been rare in any navy.

In 1880 Chief Engineer King described her as being second only to the *Trenton* amongst American cruising ships, but the hurricane that hit Apia in 1889 was an unfair stress—only HMS *Calliope*, with three times her power, escaped. For nearly twelve hours the *Vandalia* steamed

gamely to her anchors, but was eventually forced ashore and sank to her hammock-rails. Captain Schoonmaker, three officers and thirty-nine men were lost. The rest took to the rigging till the *Trenton* fetched up alongside.

From the second photograph it will be seen that the *Vandalia* was of conventional old-fashioned appearance with a full ship rig and a knee, or clipper-like, bow. The fancy framing of the two forward ports on the gundeck, unoccupied by guns, also appears in some other American ships here. We do not recall having seen it elsewhere.

HMS *Boadicea* 1875-1905

Iron Screw Corvette, cased with wood
(later, Screw Cruiser, 2nd Class)

In HMS *Boadicea* and her two sisters, Nathaniel Barnaby, who succeeded Reed after an interregnum under a Council of Construction, arrived at an interesting halfway stage in cruiser development. Like the screw frigates she followed, the *Boadicea* was single-screwed and ship-rigged, handled from aft, and carried her main armament in broadside batteries between decks. On the other hand, though sheathed with wood and coppered, she was iron in frame and shell, with the watertight hull subdivision impossible in a wooden warship. Her guns were muzzle-loading, but being forged and rifled, and mounted on iron carriages and slides, were a marked advance on cast-iron smoothbores on wooden truck carriages, and she was armed with torpedoes. Perhaps her most striking progress, however, lay in compound engines and high-pressure boilers that enabled her to cross the Atlantic under steam alone, with something to spare.

Launched in Portsmouth Dockyard in 1875, she displaced 3,932 tons, was 280ft long and 45ft beam, with 23ft draught. She had fourteen 7in and two 6in RML guns, and two 14in Whitehead torpedo-launching carriages. She rode well and handled easily, but was only moderate under sail.

Her photograph (taken in mid-career, for she was originally black) shows her knee bow carrying the figure of the Queen of the Iceni. The garland shown in the photograph (taken in Portsmouth in April 1883) was for the wedding of her gunnery officer, who became Admiral Sir Reginald Tupper. Her sisters and most later ships had square stems or rams. When she joined a miscellaneous fleet assembled at Portland against a Russian threat in 1878, and other ships exercised 'Prepare to ram', the *Boadicea* individually was ordered to 'Prepare to bump'.

After that alarm subsided, Commodore Frederick Richards (known, though not to his face, as 'King Dick') took her out to the Cape. When he was relieved by Rear-Admiral Noel Salmon VC the *Boadicea* was recommissioned on the station and completed seven years there, the first five without docking. In 1885 she was refitted and partly rearmed at Portsmouth, after which she had two commissions on the East Indies station as flagship, wearing the flags of Admirals Fremantle, Robinson and Kennedy, successively. Both at the Cape and on this station she lent a hand with minor wars ashore.

On relief by HMS *Bonaventure* in 1894 she went into Class 4 Reserve till 1905 when she was one of the long list of ships disposed of by order of the First Sea Lord, Sir John Fisher.

USS *Trenton* 1876-89

Wooden Screw Corvette, 1st Rate

(Screw Steamer, 2nd Rate - Chief Eng King, 1880.
Frigate-built Cruiser - Brassey's *Annual*, 1887)

The *Trenton*, variously classified as above, was the largest of eight ships authorised by Congress in February 1873, with the proviso that in aggregate they should not exceed 8,000 tons displacement nor $3,200,200 in cost. Launched in New York Navy Yard in 1876, the *Trenton*, 253ft long and 49ft in beam, displaced 3,900 tons—nearly half the meagre total. Her main armament consisted of eleven 8in muzzle-loading rifled guns, mounted four each side on the gun deck, and two forward and one aft on the spar deck above as chase guns. Four light saluting guns were also mounted on the spar deck amidships. Her photograph barely indicates the beginning of a ram projecting 8ft forward below the waterline. It was hoped that if it broke off after impaling an enemy, the *Trenton* would not leak too much. She had a three-cylinder compound engine, developing 3,100ihp, with a maximum speed of 13 knots; and a full ship rig spreading 24,148sq ft of canvas.

In his *Steam Navy of the United States*, Bennett says she was 'for many years after her completion the most formidable cruising ship in our neglected navy, and the only one that in type and armament at all approached the practice of other navies'. In consequence, she was regularly employed as a flagship.

In 1889, wearing the flag of Rear-Admiral L. A. Kimberly, she was in Apia, Samoa, with the US Ships *Vandalia* and *Nipsic*, HMS *Calliope* (qv) and three Germans. When a hurricane struck she was quickly in trouble. As the photograph shows, her hawsepipes were very low, on the berth deck, well below the decorated forward port on the gundeck, and seas surging through them extinguished the boilers early on. Thereafter she continued to drag slowly in the fairway. As the *Calliope* inched her way past her, Kimberly shouted 'Good luck!' and the *Trenton*'s crew gave her a generous cheer. At one stage they were sent into the rigging to act as a sail, to assist in clearing the most dangerous reef. Eventually, with ensign flying at Kimberly's insistence, though the gale was whipping bunting to shreds, she settled alongside the *Vandalia* and, sinking only to gundeck level, was able to receive her survivors. She lost only one man, killed when a port was bashed in, but both ships were a total loss.

USS *Ranger 1876-1958*

Iron Gun Boat

The United States Navy gun boat *Ranger*, the fourth naval ship to bear the name, was built of iron by Harlan and Hollingsworth at Wilmington, Delaware, between 1873 and 1876. With two sisters, she was amongst the ships authorised with the *Trenton* in 1873, the tonnage limitation having been somewhat increased. She was rigged as a three-masted barque with the old-fashioned deep single topsails, and equipped with a horizontal compound steam engine giving her a speed of about 10 knots. At one period she was armed with one 11in gun, two 9in muzzle-loaders and one 60-pounder.

First employed in the Atlantic, when she was a year old she was transferred to the Pacific and employed principally on survey duties. In 1899 in the course of an extensive refit her rig was altered to that shown in the photograph, a barquentine with standing gaffs and brailing mainsail and mizzen. She was then stationed in the Philippines where she acted as a mother ship to destroyers. On her return to the Boston Navy Yard in 1908 she was navigated on the long passage by Lt Chester W. Nimitz, thirty-five years later to command United States forces in the successful conclusion of the Pacific War.

In 1909 the *Ranger* was transferred from the United States Navy to the State of Massachusetts to act as a sea-going schoolship. In this role she regularly crossed the Atlantic to Europe, carrying over a hundred young men who gained experience both of handling a square-rigged vessel—for she navigated under sails alone for almost a third of her time—and of a coal-burning steamer with a reciprocating engine, and she became very well known in Britain. During her career as a schoolship she bore the names successively of *Nantucket*, *Rockport*, *Nantucket* again, then *Bay State* and finally *Emery Rice*. In 1932 she was again re-rigged as a barque in order to increase her usefulness as a training ship. She carried studdingsails—the sails set from studdingsail booms (extension to the yards of the foremast) used by clippers and packet ships of the nineteenth century—and she was probably the last vessel in the western world ever to set such sails as part of her working equipment. The studdingsail booms can be seen in the photograph as can also the square spritsail she could set under her bowsprit. At the end of World War II the *Ranger* became a floating museum and in this role she survived until 1958.

HMS *Inflexible 1876-1903*

Double-Screw Iron Turret Ship, Armour-plated
(later Twin-Screw Battleship, 1st Class, Armoured; and finally 2nd Class)

The *Inflexible* was a phenomenon among British battleships of this experimental period. Her size, cost, weight of armament and complexity made a great impression, but it faded rapidly until she was eventually branded by a critic as 'one of the worst designs ever inflicted upon the Navy'. One may wonder, however, whether anyone could have done much better than Barnaby in matching the Italian battleship *Duilio*'s giant guns and heavy armour within the limits of contemporary technique, tonnage and finance.

So thick was the necessary armour that only the central section of the ship could be fully protected. This citadel enclosing the machinery spaces and magazines had up to 24in of armour with massive teak backing. Upon it, four 80 ton 16in guns were mounted in two turrets, with steel-faced ('compound') armour. They were disposed *en echelon* to give maximum arcs of fire, and were hydraulically trained. They were power-loaded in a fixed position under cover of an armoured glacis above the upper deck. Before and abaft the citadel, protection depended upon a 3in armoured deck below the waterline, compartmentation, and coal, cork and canvas stowed so as to minimise flooding. Her light guns were insignificant, but her torpedo armament looked formidable—two unique submerged training tubes, two above-water carriages, and dropping devices, visible in the photograph, at bow and stern. Her heavy brig rig was for exercise and training only and in emergency could be jettisoned before action. Other innovations included the two torpedo-boats stowed on her superstructure aft, anti-rolling tanks and electric lighting. All these added up to 11,880 tons displacement. Her 320ft length and 75ft beam meant an unusual ratio of nearly 4:1. Compound engines by Elder & Co with steam from 12 boilers at 60lb gave her about $13\frac{1}{2}$ knots on service, in early life.

Launched by Portsmouth Dockyard in 1876, her completion was much delayed by modification and by criticism from Reed, who saw no merit in any design since his own resignation. She was commissioned in 1881 by Captain J. A. Fisher, appointed as the man most likely to make her work, and he handled her creditably at the bombardment of Alexandria the following year. But though he was so captivated by her ingenuity that he incorporated some of her major weaknesses in his own dreadnoughts, his successor thought it 'curious that a ship should be designed to do what she so obviously could not'. She returned full of defects in 1885, had her yards and sails replaced by fighting tops and went into reserve. She appeared at the 1887 Jubilee Review and for manoeuvres, but did only one more seagoing commission, again in the Mediterranean. She was sold in 1903.

HMS *Cormorant* 1877-1949

Composite Sloop

Though a drydock was promised in the agreement by which British Columbia entered the Dominion of Canada in 1871, for years ships could still be docked only at Mare Island, San Francisco, subject always to American permission and substantial payment. On 20 July 1887, however, in the presence of Lieutenant-Governor H. H. Nelson and Rear-Admiral Sir Michael Culme-Seymour, Miss Kathleen O'Reilly cut a blue ribbon and HMS *Cormorant*'s entry opened the Esquimalt drydock. Astern of her in the photograph is HMS *Triumph*, Sir Michael's flagship, painted white for a tropical cruise.

The *Cormorant* belonged to a class of fourteen sloops, all launched between 1876 and 1880, with a designed displacement of 1,130 tons, 170ft long, 36ft in breadth and 16ft draught. Early

ships of the class, including the *Cormorant*, had what Admiral Ballard calls 'a knee bow of clipper cut'. The others had square stems. Their composite construction gave them strength and a potentially long life. They were relatively well-armed, very handy and extremely seaworthy, but their speed was inadequate for much more than imperial policing and 'consular' duties. In this capacity, however, ten out of the fourteen sisters served effectively on the Pacific station. (The ten included HMS *Doterel* destroyed by an accidental explosion in Magellan Straits in 1881 on her way out to the station.)

With two exceptions these ships were built in royal dockyards, the *Cormorant* coming from Chatham where she was launched in September 1877. Her Humphrys and Tennant compound engines and three cylindrical double-ended boilers working at 60lb developed 950ihp, giving 11.8 knots on trials. She was barque rigged. Unlike her sisters who hoisted their screw on making sail, she had a feathering device for reducing propeller drag. Despite having a light poop and topgallant forecastle, accommodation was cramped since machinery spaces occupied the middle section of her hull. She retained her original two 7in and four 64-pounder MLR guns throughout her seagoing life, which ran only to two commissions.

Her first, in Australian waters, lasted nearly 4½ years, during which period she assisted in punishing some murderous natives in the New Hebrides. On return in 1882 she had a long refit and a spell in reserve until 1885. She was next commissioned by Commander J. E. T. Nicolls for the Pacific. Twenty-five years later her then First Lieutenant became Director of the Naval Service of Canada, retiring as Admiral Sir Charles Kingsmill.

After this commission she was dismantled and sent out to Gibraltar as an accommodation ship. In 1900 she became the base name ship, flying the flag of the Admiral Superintendent, and continued, with her name changed to *Rooke* in 1946, until broken up in 1949. She was outlived by three sisters, including the *Gannet* still afloat in 1972.

HMS *Comus* 1878–1904

Steel Screw Corvette (later 3rd Class Cruiser)

This photograph shows HMS *Comus* leaving San Francisco 16 September 1882 with HRH Princess Louise, fourth daughter of Queen Victoria, with her husband, the Marquis of Lorne, Governor-General of Canada, for passage to Esquimalt. The ship is dressed with masthead flags, the Royal Standard at the main.

The *Comus*, launched and completed by John Elder of Govan in 1878, was the name ship of a class of nine, all with names beginning with 'C'. Before her completion a committee simplifying the classification of HM ships decided these were 3rd class cruisers, but concealed this so effectively in a confidential book that the editor of the Navy List was not informed. Consequently they remained 'corvettes', for most practical purposes, for many years.

Designed by Barnaby for foreign service, the *Comus* was 225ft long, 44½ft beam and displaced 2,380 tons. A steel hull (cased in wood and copper-sheathed) and a 1½in armoured deck covering her vitals were then recent innovations in the Royal Navy. Compound engines developed power

for 13 knots and 470 tons of coal gave her a nominal radius of 3,800 miles. Her full ship rig was later altered to a barque. Breech-loading guns being still out of favour, she was originally armed with two 7in and twelve 64-pounder MLR guns. These were eventually replaced by ten new type breech-loaders and two torpedo-launching carriages were added.

A sister was described as 'a wonderful little ship . . . as self-contained as a ship could possibly be'. Well-armed, she could also carry and lay mines, and land nearly two hundred armed men with a field-gun. She held six months' provisions and used only salt water in her boilers. Her 500 tons of coal were used only when necessary. 'It would be hard to imagine a ship more scientifically equipped for . . . trade protection and Empire policing'.

Commissioned first in 1879 for China, the *Comus* was summoned across the Pacific to allow Lord Lorne to pacify British Columbia. Having joined the Dominion of Canada in 1871 without universal enthusiasm, the province was now aggrieved by the delay in completing the Canadian Pacific Railway that had obliged the Lornes to travel by an American railway to San Francisco. The *Comus* returned them there in December after a mission that left a more contented province to await the CPR's arrival in 1885.

The ship's further service included two and a half commissions on the North American station and another one in the Pacific. She was sold for breaking-up in 1904.

HMS *Amphion* 1883-1906

Steel Cruiser 2nd Class

This splendid photograph, taken from Grant Knoll at the NW corner of the old Esquimalt Dockyard, shows HMS *Amphion*, with paying-off pendant streaming from her main masthead, being seen off by some friends, including a girl who seems to be playing a flute as well as waving

a handkerchief. The date is presumably 1890, for although the commission had still to be completed elsewhere, she discarded sails after it, long before her next visit to Esquimalt.

Her three sisters, *Arethusa*, *Leander* and *Phaeton* (all well known in the Pacific) were contract-built by Napier on the Clyde, but the *Amphion* was allocated to Pembroke Dockyard to use spare capacity there. They were a notable advance towards a cruiser of moderate size with the speed, strength and endurance needed for fleet work and on ocean trade routes. Technical progress allowed them steel hulls, until recently considered too expensive and of uncertain quality. 315ft long, 40ft beam, and of 4,300 tons displacement, they carried ten 6in BLR guns, fourteen light ones and four torpedo-launching carriages. Compound engines by Maudslay developing 5,550ihp gave the *Amphion* 17 knots trial speed. A 1½in armoured deck covered machinery spaces and magazines, and though 1,000 tons of coal gave a nominal radius of 11,000 miles at 10 knots, barquentine rig was provided to save fuel.

The *Amphion* was commissioned for Queen Victoria's Jubilee Review in 1887 and took part in the 1888 manoeuvres, after which an appraising committee of three admirals recommended removing the square yards on her foremast to save topweight, but Sir Arthur Hood, a diehard First Sea Lord, disagreed. In December 1888 Captain E. G. Hulton commissioned her for the Pacific. Her lieutenants included the future Admiral Sir George Warrender and Captain Robert Falcon Scott of the Antarctic. On 6 November 1889, while taking the Governor-General, Lord Stanley, to Vancouver, she was holed on a reef in Haro Strait and had to return to Esquimalt for repairs. In 1890 she was transferred to the Mediterranean for the second half of the commission. Three years later, again in the Mediterranean, she saw the fleet flagship, the *Victoria*, rammed and sunk by the *Camperdown* off Tripoli, Syria.

She was twice more commissioned for the Pacific, in 1897 by Captain F. Finnis, leaving Esquimalt, towards its end, on 26 August 1899; and in 1900 by Captain John Casement. Her duties then included escorting the Duke and Duchess of York from Vancouver to Victoria in October 1901 and the destroyers *Virago* and *Sparrowhawk* to Honolulu, en route to China, in 1903. She paid off for the last time in April 1904 and was sold in 1906.

HMS *Imperieuse* 1883-1913

Steel Twin-Screw Armour-plated Barbette Ship
(later Twin-Screw Cruiser, 1st Class, Armoured)

With her sister the *Warspite*, HMS *Imperieuse* constituted the last attempt to combine full square rig with advanced technical developments in a large ship. It was unsuccessful and supports the critics who hold that the Admiralty was less to blame for a cautious initial approach to 'steam navigation' than for protracting the last stage of transition. Barnaby, their designer, described these sisters as being intended, 'especially for foreign stations, where fast unarmoured ships may have to be opposed and where the second-class ironclads of an enemy may have to be met and engaged'. Their requirements included a speed of 16 knots, powerful armament, good armour protection, a large coal supply plus auxiliary sail power to conserve it, and a sheathed and coppered bottom.

Launched at Portsmouth in 1883, modifications during building delayed her completion and added greatly to her displacement, which came out at 8,500 tons on a length of 315ft and 62ft beam, but compound engines of 8,000ihp achieved her intended 16 knots. Four 9.2in guns were

new in both pattern and disposition, which followed French lines in placing them singly, forward, aft and on each beam, revolving inside fixed armoured barbettes with only a 2in shield on the gun. Exceptional tumble home failed to give the beam guns ahead or astern fire without unacceptable blast damage, and weight would only permit three 6in guns each side. Protection was reasonably generous and they carried six 18in torpedo tubes.

The photograph shows her in 1886 when commissioned for trials. These proved that her brig rig was rather worse than useless, and her masts and yards were replaced by a single 'military' mast amidships. She had a radius of 5,500 miles at 10 knots without them.

After the Jubilee Review of 1887 she went into reserve, but in 1889 was recommissioned for China where she bore the flags of Sir Frederick Richards and Sir Edmund Fremantle before being relieved in 1894. A subsequent refit increased her secondary armament to ten 6in guns. In 1896 she hoisted the flag of Rear-Admiral H. St L. B. Palliser for the Pacific station and next year had the unusual duty of assisting his search for treasure reputedly buried on Cocos Island, without success. In 1899 she was paid off and refitted, and apart from the 1903 manoeuvres was either in reserve or employed in harbour service, for a time under the name of *Sapphire II*. She was condemned in 1912 and sold next year.

HMS *Calliope 1884-1951*

Steel Screw Corvette
(later, 3rd Class Cruiser)

HMS *Calliope*, launched in Portsmouth Dockyard on 24 June 1884 by Lady Phipps Hornby, wife of the Commander-in-Chief, was a slightly larger version of the *Comus*, already described. Similarly built of steel, wood and copper-sheathed, an extra 10ft in length gave her a displacement of 2,770 tons. More powerful Rennie engines added a knot or more and she had a feathering instead of a hoisting screw. Production of breech-loading guns allowed her to be armed with four 6in and twelve 5in BLR guns, and she had a barque rig from the start.

Commissioned in January 1887 by Captain R. C. Kane for service in China, she was diverted to the Australian station in September. The photograph shows her opening the Calliope Dock in Auckland, New Zealand, in 1888. Sharing the dock astern of her and also dressed with masthead flags is HMS *Diamond*, the last wooden ship of sloop status or above to be launched in a royal dockyard.

In January 1889 the *Calliope* went to Samoa where, in a tense situation created by conflicting German and American interests, Kane boldly intervened to forestall more than one German coup, and American men-of-war manned yards in his honour. On 16 March a violent typhoon swept Apia harbour and every ship was in difficulty. Kane slipped his last remaining anchor and, with full power on the engines barely giving steering way, worked the *Calliope* out to windward, cheered by the American flagship *Trenton* (qv) as she scraped by. The six American and German men-of-war present all dragged ashore, four of them permanently, with loss of life. The American

Admiral, Kimberly, wrote to Kane: 'It was a gallant thing, and you did it so well that it could not have been done better. We could not have been gladder if it had been one of our own ships, for in a time like that I can truly say with our old admiral, Josiah Tattnall that "blood is thicker than water".' In the last resort, however, all depended on her engines, and her Engineer Officer, Mr H. G. Bourke, very properly received immediate promotion.

When she paid off in April 1890 the *Calliope* had covered 76,814 nautical miles in 663 days at sea, against 528 in harbour, during that commission.

For various reasons, she remained in reserve until 1897 when she was commissioned as a sail training ship for several years. In 1907 she was towed to the Tyne and became training ship for the local RNVR Division. In 1914 she was renamed *Helicon* to release '*Calliope*' to a new light cruiser and extended her duties to include acting as a recruiting depot for the Royal Naval Division. In 1931 she resumed her own name until sold in 1951.

HMS *Racer 1884–1928*

Composite Screw Sloop

Six ships of the *Reindeer* class were laid down in 1882–3 as gun vessels but were re-classified by an Admiralty Order of November 1884 as sloops. HMS *Racer* was one of the four built in the Royal Dockyard at Devonport, where she was launched in 1884.

She had a composite hull and was of 970 tons displacement, 167ft in length, 32ft in breadth, and drew 13ft. Her engines, supplied by Hawthorn Leslie, gave 920ihp and a trial speed of 11½ knots, and she carried 150 tons of coal. *Brassey* credits this with providing a radius of 2,300 miles but such estimates were notoriously optimistic, largely through making insufficient allowance for auxiliary services. She carried eight 5in BL guns, four on each side, and eight light weapons.

Commissioned in April 1885, she joined the Channel Squadron for a preliminary work-up before going out to the Cape of Good Hope and West Coast of Africa station. There in 1886 she took part in a punitive expedition in the Niger, and in 1887 assisted in operations in defence of Suakin against dervish forces. At this time, on medical advice, a commission was often divided between African service and another station, and the *Racer* completed this one in the Mediterranean. Her second commission was similarly split between the Cape and the South-east Coast of America stations.

In 1894 she went into reserve at Devonport until 1897, when she was commissioned as a tender to HMS *Britannia*, a first-rate hulked at Dartmouth with the *Hindostan*, where newly-entered naval cadets were trained. The *Racer*, of course, was to give them at least a taste of sail training. In 1903, when Admiral Fisher as 2nd Sea Lord induced the Admiralty to lower the age of entry and replace the *Britannia* by two naval colleges ashore, the *Racer* was allocated to the one at Osborne in the Isle of Wight where the young gentlemen (aged 12 to 13) went for 2½ years before going on to Dartmouth. Officers of the college were borne on her books. The photograph shows her employed in this role which continued until World War I, a struggle which showed once more that some use can be found for almost any vessel that is not too extravagant in upkeep and manpower.

The *Racer* and her three surviving sisters were converted to salvage vessels. After the war she continued salvage work and from 1920 to 1925 assisted in recovering the gold lost in the liner *Laurentic*, mined off Ireland on passage to America. She was finally sold in 1928.

USS *Atlanta* 1884-1912

Steel Protected Cruiser

The *Atlanta* and her sister *Boston*, along with the larger *Chicago* and the small despatch vessel *Dolphin*, were the four ships authorised by Congress in 1883 that formed the beginning of the new American Navy. The *Atlanta* is seen here weighing her port anchor, with a hose washing the cable and plenty of steam from the capstan engine. Two purchases over the side are ready to lift the close-stowing anchor up to its bed on the forecastle edge. Amongst points worth notice are the decorative work on the bow, the design of the starboard anchor, the heavy brig rig, and the 'military' tops, still platforms for light weapons and marksmen rather than for fire control. The thirty-eight stars on the jack would seem to place the date not later than 1889, since the admission of four more states to the Union that year would make the number 42.

The design of the *Atlanta* and *Boston* owed something to two young naval architects who, after leaving Annapolis, had done a course at the Royal Naval College, Greenwich. There they had a look at developments that had arisen in Europe during the long American holiday from new construction.

All four ships were allocated to John Roach & Son, of Chester, Pennsylvania, but his reach had exceeded his grasp and the cruisers had to be completed in naval yards. Their hulls were

steel and an armoured deck shielding their machinery spaces from plunging fire made them 'protected' cruisers, as distinct from 'armoured' cruisers which had vertical side armour as well. The *Atlanta*'s displacement was 3,189 tons, length 270ft, and beam 42ft. As originally armed, she mounted an 8in BLR gun forward and aft, the bow gun to port and the stern gun to starboard of the centre line, and three 6in guns on either side between them. Her engines developed 3,500ihp on one shaft, giving her perhaps 16 knots and a 5,000 mile radius at economical speed.

She was first commissioned in 1886, and in 1889 joined the other three of the group in a Squadron of Evolution, commonly known as 'the White Squadron', from the colour of their hulls, or 'the ABCDs', from their initial letters. They did a great deal of cruising and exercising together, gaining valuable experience and showing the flag. The *Atlanta* seems to have had her share of the teething troubles that are apt to arise in a new design, and after her first commissions spent a good deal of time in navy yards. In the mid–90s she was unrigged and underwent other forms of modernisation. Her last full sea-going commission was spent in the South Atlantic and Caribbean in 1901–4. She then served as a barracks ship for torpedo craft at Norfolk till 1909, and at Charleston till 1912, when she was sold.

USS *Chicago 1885-1936*

Steel Protected Cruiser

Designed by Naval Constructor Josiah Fernald, the *Chicago* was launched by John Roach but completed in a navy yard, like the *Atlanta*. She displaced 4,500 tons, was 328ft long and 48ft in beam. She was originally armed with four 8in guns in sponsons on upper deck level, eight 6in on the main deck and two 5in well aft on that level. Her original machinery was remarkable, one vertical compound engine on either side driving the opposite shaft by means of an overhead ('walking') beam. These developed 5,000ihp and a speed of 15 knots. Early plans show a protective deck over machinery spaces only: this may be an error or it may have been extended later, during modernisation. As her photograph shows, she was barque-rigged and looks a good deal more solid than the *Atlanta*.

Four years after her launch, she was first commissioned on 17 April 1889 by Captain H. B. Robeson to become flagship of the Squadron of Evolution, and remained in constant demand as a flagship. Whether due to better design, larger size, more experience, time in building, good fortune or a combination of these, she had a much more active and lengthy career than the *Atlanta*. In 1893 she was present at an international Naval Review at Hampton Roads to commemorate Columbus. In 1893-5 when she was flagship of the European Squadron, the flag-captain was A. T. Mahan, a historian who influenced history and a prophet greatly honoured abroad, though his admiral seems to have had, without justification, the practical man's distrust of a theorist.

After paying off on her return, she was extensively modernised. Sails were discarded, triple-expansion engines raised her ihp to 9,000 and her speed to 18 knots, and four 8in guns of new pattern and fourteen 5in QF guns replaced her original armament. This restored her to flagship status for another ten years.

From 1908 she was assigned to training duties until America entered World War I in April 1917, when she became flagship of the Submarine Force Atlantic, with the future Fleet Admiral Chester Nimitz as the admiral's aide and Chief of Staff. In December 1919, Nimitz rejoined her, this time commanding Submarine Division 14, at Pearl Harbor.

On 30 September 1923, she was decommissioned there but continued in reduced circumstances as a barracks ship (under the name *Alton* from 1928) until May 1936, when she was sold. She avoided the ignominy of being broken up by foundering in mid-Pacific in July, whilst on tow to San Francisco.

HMS *Wasp 1886-7*

Composite Screw Gunboat, 1st Class

Among the last designs by Barnaby, whose cross had been both heavy and splintered to a degree unusual even for Directors of Naval Construction, was a class of four gunboats which included the *Wasp*. They were intended to meet Lord Charles Beresford's criticism of their predecessors as being weak and slow. Displacing 715 tons, with a length of 165ft, a beam of 29ft, and maximum draught of 13ft, they approached the dimensions of a gun vessel of a decade earlier and engines of 1,000ihp increased their speed to 13 knots. Three 4in breech-loading guns were mounted on each side. Two were abreast on the forecastle, and the others in sponsons just forward of the main and mizzen masts are clearly shown in her photograph. Though lighter than the muzzle-loading guns in earlier gunboats, they had a much better rate of fire and greater accuracy. Admiral Ballard says the Navy then called the *Wasp* a three-masted brigantine—but most of us would now describe her as a barquentine.

Launched on the Tyne by Armstrong Mitchell on 13 September 1886, she was commissioned for the China station and sailed from Sheerness on 30 May 1887. Between Singapore and Hong Kong she disappeared and it was presumed that she had been lost in a typhoon which swept the South China Sea on 17 September 1887.

Since the last *Wasp* had been wrecked on Tory Island only three years before many seamen deemed the name unlucky. Other thinkers, despite the absence of any evidence whatever, placed the blame firmly on such factors as lack of seamanship, inadequate complement, or more commonly, poor design. The Admiralty, naturally, would have none of this: after full consideration they declared the *Wasp* to be an improvement on preceding types. It would be presumption to challenge their verdict. Between the Crimean programme and the *Wasp*, over 170 masted sloops, gun vessels and gunboats had shown the flag all over the world in all weathers and not one other had succumbed to the elements alone. What higher tribute to designers, builders, seamen and engineers could be offered?

HMS *Beagle 1889-1905*

Steel Twin-Screw Sloop

William White who succeeded Barnaby in 1885 followed the same general policy in regard to sloops. White's biographer explains that for service on stations like the Pacific, with immense distances and limited maintenance and docking facilities, more emphasis was placed on sail power and hence a single screw was called for, twin screws being incompatible with good sailing qualities. Elsewhere, in China for example, moderate draught and twin screws were acceptable, with sail playing only a minor part. In both cases, however, the hulls had to be wood sheathed and coppered against fouling and the boilers to be capable of continuous steaming and easily accessible for repairs, which ruled out great speeds.

The *Beagle* and her sister *Basilisk*, in the second category, differed from Barnaby's last sloop, the *Swallow* of 1885, in having a steel hull, sheathed and coppered, and slightly more power. Their displacement was 1,170 tons, length 195ft, beam 28ft and they drew 12½ft. They had eight 5in BLR guns, four each side, and Rennie triple-expansion engines developing 2,000ihp on twin screws gave 14½ knots on trials. The photograph shows their barquentine rig with pole topmasts.

Launched at Portsmouth in February 1889, she was commissioned in 1893 by Commander R. Neeld for the South-east Coast of America station. Roger Keyes—the future Admiral of the Fleet, Lord Keyes—who joined her as a newly promoted lieutenant described her as 'lightly rigged and a very poor sailer, but we treated her as a sailing ship wherever possible'.

In 1883 she was bought by Trinder Anderson and Company who had entered into an returned to South America for a second time, relieving the *Barracouta*. Commander D. A. Gamble 'always did things in dashing style' and was promoted towards the end of the commission, after which she went into reserve at Portsmouth. Her third commission, at the Cape, was cut short by her inclusion in Sir John Fisher's sweeping reductions of minor ships on foreign stations in order to concentrate strength at home to meet the growing threat from Tirpitz's new German Navy. She was sold in July 1905.

For five years no more sloops followed the *Beagles* but the Admiralty then resumed a modest programme that just carried auxiliary sail into the twentieth century. HMS *Shearwater* was one of the penultimate class of six, and was built in Sheerness Dockyard. Her chief difference from the *Beagle* lay in her armament of six 4in quick-firing guns instead of eight 5in BL which allowed a reduced tonnage without decreased volume of fire. She was 180ft long, 33ft beam and displaced 980 tons. She had engines from the Thames Iron Works and Belleville water-tube boilers giving 1100ihp and a speed of 12.6 knots. It will be seen that she was rigged like the *Beagle* but had a comparatively elaborate bridge just before the mizzenmast.

On 24 October 1901, she commissioned at Chatham for the Pacific and after sailing never returned under the White Ensign. In 1905 Fisher withdrew the Pacific Squadron, bar the *Shearwater*, whose captain, Commander A. T. Hunt, became 'Commander-in-charge for station duties on the west coast of North America'. She normally patrolled northward in summer, keeping an eye on the seal fisheries, and in winter went southward to Mexico and Central America. In 1908 HMS *Algerine*, a sloop of the preceding class, was transferred from China to share the load. In 1910 the Canadian Government bought two elderly cruisers, HM ships *Niobe* and *Rainbow*, to start a Canadian Navy. The smaller arrived in Esquimalt as HMCS *Rainbow* on 7 November. Two days later control of the dockyard was transferred to the new Service, but it continued to maintain the *Shearwater* and *Algerine* for the Royal Navy. Legend says they enjoyed a glorious brief spell of virtual independence, unfettered by wireless, offering unlimited scope for sport.

In early 1914, however, they joined an international force keeping an eye on side-effects of the Mexican civil war. When European war came, with the modern German light cruiser *Leipzig* in the area, there was great anxiety for the sloops. Most gallantly, the poorly-armed, partly manned *Rainbow* went south to cover them, and providentially no contact was made.

With von Spee's squadron at large and the Royal Navy's Pacific Squadron gone, the British Columbian coast looked vulnerable, and Sir Richard McBride, the provincial premier, on his own initiative bought two submarines building for Chile in Seattle. Lieutenant Adrian Keyes, RN, Roger's brother who had retired in Canada, trained volunteer crews, and the *Shearwater* (minus her ship's company, sent east to Halifax) was lent as depot ship to the new submarines CC1 and CC2. In 1915 she was formally transferred to the Royal Canadian Navy and in 1917 escorted the submarines to the East Coast via Panama. Sold in May 1922, she became the merchant ship *Vedas* until 1935.

Merchant Vessels

Iris 1842-57

Wooden Paddle Steam Packet

This photograph is the earliest known to the authors of a British built merchant paddle steamer. It was taken in Aalborg Harbour, Denmark, probably in 1843 and the original is in the Maritime Museum in the Kronborg Castle at Elsinore, Denmark. It is reproduced here by kind permission of the Director of that institution, Dr Henning Henningsen. The vessel is the *Iris* built by James and William Hall at Aberdeen in 1842. She is a good example of a packet steamer of this early period when steamships could still be profitably employed only on short packet routes and on the subsidised North Atlantic service. Note the quarter galleries. She was 173ft long and her engines, built by William Simpson and Company of Aberdeen, drove paddles over 18ft in diameter.

Shortly after she was built the *Iris* was sold for £10,000 to the Aalborg Steamship Company and for fifteen years she sailed in Danish waters, mainly between Aalborg and Copenhagen on a regular service providing, of course, by far the fastest and most reliable service between these two cities. The business was at first very profitable and in 1848 the Aalborg Steamship Company paid a dividend of 27½ per cent and were encouraged to buy a second Aberdeen-built vessel, the *Juno*.

The *Iris* was a long, narrow, sharp vessel whose general shape, like that of some other early steamers, the *Great Britain* among them, appears to have anticipated the fast sailing ships of the 1850s. She had berths for thirty male passengers in a large saloon and for twelve females in a much smaller cabin forward. She also had a restaurant and space for carrying cargo and for the cattle which were one of the main sources of her income. The master lived in the small cabin in the after end of the starboard sponson. The mate had a somewhat smaller space on the other side. The whale-backed deckhouses clearly visible in the photograph immediately forward of the paddles contained the accommodation of the engineers. The crew lived in an under-deck forecastle.

The *Iris* was rigged with a stumpy schooner rig (the top masts are housed in the photograph), with a long bowsprit and jibboom. She was a handsome little vessel and the photograph brings out very well the simplicity of these early powered ships. She was painted on a number of occasions and there are several pictures of her in Denmark, one showing her with King Christian VII on board a few days before she started work in regular service. The service in which she ran ceased to be economic in the 1850s and the company which owned her went into liquidation in 1857.

Great Britain 1843- *Still in Existence*

Iron Screw Steam Passenger Vessel

The *Great Britain* was a unique landmark in the history of marine engineering and of naval architecture. She was the first large vessel in which two of the three essential prerequisites of the successful steamship were brought together. She had an iron hull and a screw propeller. The third ingredient for viability, an economical engine, was to come twenty years later. She was

also the first large iron ship, the largest ship of her age and a vessel whose design was remarkably different in many respects from anything which had gone before. Her hull form anticipated the fast sailing vessels of the 1850s and 1860s which began with the great American clippers and incorporated structural features which were to have considerable influence on shipbuilding. She was, of course, the product of the genius of Isambard Kingdom Brunel, but the idea of fitting her with screw propulsion came not from him but from a board of directors. They had been impressed with the success of the screw steamship *Archimedes* which in 1840 had circumnavigated Britain and made the fastest passage to that date from Britain to Oporto. The *Great Britain*'s original engine was of 1,000 nominal horsepower and the four cylinders of 7ft 4in diameter had a 6ft stroke. They drove the propeller through a chain drive that was taken right up to the level of the upper deck. The engine was in fact an adapted paddle installation.

This photograph, taken by Fox Talbot, was made by direct enlargement from the original calleotype negative which is one of the treasures of the National Maritime Museum. It is quite possible that this is the first photograph ever taken of a ship of any kind. It shows the vessel shortly after her launch lying in Bristol docks. As can be seen, she was rigged as a six-masted schooner, anticipating the pioneer American vessel of this rig, usually spoken of as the world's first, the *George W. Wells*, by fifty-seven years. The rig proved extremely economical in manpower and maintenance costs and was very efficient. The *Great Britain*, despite her great size, handled excellently under sail.

The beauty of her lines is apparent even in this very early photograph. After a number of voyages in the North Atlantic trade, the *Great Britain* had a long and highly successful career sailing between Britain and Australia, broken by trooping during the Crimean War and the Indian Mutiny. At this period of her career she was equipped with a power unit of twin oscillating cylinders geared to the propeller shaft. This unit, built by John Penn & Sons of Greenwich, developed 500 nominal horsepower. She had been re-rigged in 1853 as a full-rigged ship. In the Australian trade she was operated as an auxiliary steamship, that is, she sailed for long distances without using her engines.

In 1886, after damage off Cape Horn, she was made into a storage hulk in the Falkland Islands. In 1969 she was still lying there and in 1970 this landmark in the history of ships was brought back to Bristol, England, where she is now being slowly restored.

Fulton 1856-70

Wooden Paddle Steam Passenger Liner

The *Fulton* was launched in 1856 in New York City, a wooden paddle steamer of 2,061 tons gross with squaresails on her two masts and with two funnels. Her machinery comprised two oscillating engines of 10ft stroke and 65in diameter, developing nearly 2,000ihp. It was built by Stillman and Allen of New York. She was designed for the trans-Atlantic service and she was, of course, virtually obsolete when she was built—almost the last British North Atlantic passenger paddle steamer, the *Persia*, had been built the year before, but of iron. Although the last great Cunard paddler the *Scotia* was to hold the 'Blue Riband' from 1862 to 1867, the day of the paddle steamer in deep-sea passenger service was already ending. The *Fulton*'s owners, the New York and Havre Steam Navigation Company, had a subsidy, at first of $200,000 a year, for operating the New York–Havre mail service via Southampton on which the *Fulton* sailed and which lasted until 1861. Then, on the outbreak of the Civil War, the *Fulton* was taken up by the US War Department as a transport.

She resumed sailings across the Atlantic in 1865 between New York and Havre via Falmouth instead of Southampton but her owners were unable to obtain a new mail subsidy from the American Government. After two years the service was abandoned and the *Fulton* was in due course chartered to the New York and Bremen Steamship Company.

In 1869 she made another Atlantic voyage to Europe via Southampton. But by now she was completely obsolete, the line which had chartered her went out of business, and next year the *Fulton*, whose wooden hull had deteriorated rapidly, probably as a result of her war service, was broken up. Her engines were still in good order and were built into another vessel.

Great Eastern 1858-91
Iron Screw and Paddle Steam Passenger Vessel

The genesis of the *Great Eastern* was in the idea of a steam vessel large enough to carry coal for a non-stop voyage to Australia, as well as a large number of passengers and a paying tonnage of cargo, despite the inefficiency of the engines of the 1850s and their prodigious fuel consumption. She was roughly six times the size of any ship built before her and her construction, which took four years, was the subject of enormous public interest and enthusiasm. It was to be forty years before her size was exceeded.

One of the principal technical problems to be solved in her design was to develop sufficient power to drive her 22,000 tons. The solution arrived at was to use two separate power systems, one to drive a screw and the other to drive paddle wheels. The four screw-engine cylinders were of 7ft bore and 4ft stroke. The paddle cylinders had a stroke of 14ft on a 6ft 2in bore and the forging of the great crank shafts of the paddles was a major engineering achievement of the age. The vessel was rigged with six masts and carried 6,500sq ft of canvas, but she used her sails very little. The hull was divided transversely into twelve watertight compartments and there were no openings in the bulkheads below the second deck. All the passenger accommodation was below the main deck and the design provided for 800 first-class, 2,000 second-class and 1,200 third-class passengers. In fact the vessel was never fitted out for anything like this number.

The Great Eastern's commercial failure is a well-known story. She was never employed in the trade for which she was designed but made her name as a cable layer. In nine years she was

responsible for five trans-Atlantic cables and one from Bombay to Suez. She was laid up for eleven years and broken up over the period 1888 to 1891. The photograph shows her laid up in Milford Haven in the last years of her life. Note the schooner lying inside her, completely dwarfed by the *Great Eastern*'s vast bulk. The small print shows the bridge during her cable-laying period. The occasion on which this photograph was taken is not known but she appears to be at sea and there are women visible in the background.

Gipsy 1859-78
Iron Screw Steam Packet

The steam and sail propelled vessel depicted here in the last days of her life was the *Gipsy*, built by Malcolmson Brothers at Waterford in 1859 of iron. Nearly 700 tons gross, she was equipped with a twin-cylinder engine of 250nhp built by Smith and Rodger of Glasgow. She ran between Bristol and Waterford in the ownership of the Waterford Steamship Company, and with her three-masted schooner rig with sails brailed-in on standing gaffs and her tall funnel she is a representative packet ship of her period. She carried over 300 people in summer conditions.

The disaster depicted in this photograph occured in 1878 when, outward bound for Waterford from Bristol, she struck one of the numerous mudbanks in the River Avon. Her passengers were taken off but on the next tide she was submerged and soon afterwards she broke her back. She blocked the channel into the docks at Bristol and five days after her stranding, during which time she was the object of enormous interest and of profit to local cabmen, she was blown up with 200lb of dynamite. Even then it was some weeks before normal navigation in the river was completely restored.

Agamemnon 1865-1907
Iron Screw Steam Cargo Vessel

The Ocean Steamship Company, parent of the Blue Funnel Line, came into existence in 1865 and in the same year three steamships of great importance in the history of the world's merchant shipping were launched for the new company. They were named *Agamemnon*, *Ajax* and *Achilles* and were all built by Scott and Company of Greenock. Each measured 209ft in length and 38ft in beam, and each was of 2,280 tons gross. Their importance rested in the fact that they were the first ocean-going steamships regularly and profitably to be employed in the long-range trades. Their success stemmed from the use of improved compound engines which enabled them to steam more economically than any of their predecessors. The engine of the *Agamemnon* developed 945ihp but occupied only 14ft of the vessel's length.

With these three steamships three technical developments of the second half of the nineteenth century were for the first time successfully combined. These were an iron hull, which because of its strength could be built with much greater length to its beam—the *Agamemnon* and her sisters for instance had a length-beam ratio of roughly 8:1—and which was lighter for its size and strength than a wooden hull, an improved screw propeller and an efficient and economical compound engine. An iron hull was really essential for a screw-driven vessel—the strains imposed by the propeller shaft's torque were too great for a normal large wooden hull if the engine was powerful enough to drive the vessel at useful speeds. These technical developments were utilised by a firm which applied relatively advanced managerial techniques in the operation of steam vessels in long-range trades.

The successful use of the *Agamemnon* and her sisters in the China trade from 1865 was the beginning of the end of the merchant sailing ship in general long-range ocean trade, and of the end of the era of steam-and-sail itself. For although the *Agamemnon* was heavily rigged as a barque the new type of compound engines were rapidly to develop to a point at which sails were necessary neither for emergencies nor for economy in fuel in normal operations. The final abandonment of sails in large vessels followed the introduction of twin screws.

The *Agamemnon* began her first voyage to China in April 1866. She and her sisters regularly steamed from Liverpool to Mauritius via the Cape of Good Hope, over 8,000 miles, without stopping, a remarkable achievement in comparison with the performance of previous steam vessels. She was given a new and even more efficient engine in 1878. Sold to a Dutch firm in 1897, she was broken up in Italy ten years later.

Natal 1866-1905

Iron Screw Steam Passenger and Cargo Vessel

The schooner-rigged steamer *Natal* of just over 600 tons was built in 1866 by Day and Summers at Southampton for the Union Steamship Company. She was an iron vessel with a compound engine, rigged as an orthodox topsail schooner and shaped very much as a three-masted iron barque of her period would have been with long narrow deep hull, curved clipper stem, figurehead, bowsprit and even a jibboom. As such she is typical of many medium-sized merchant steamships of her period.

For the first two years of her life the *Natal* ran on a Cape Town–Mauritius–Ceylon service. The Union Steamship Company then put her on the South African coastal service, in which she became very well known. The subsidised mail service at this time ran only to Cape Town. The coastal service went from there to Durban, calling at coastal ports on the way. Between 1875 and 1880 she worked a Cape Town–Zanzibar service and in 1879 was the ship which carried the captive Chief Cetewayo to Cape Town.

In 1883 she was brought by Trinder Anderson and Company who had entered into an agreement with the Government of Western Australia to provide a service to connect West Australia with Singapore, and, through transhipment at Singapore, with the Peninsular and

Oriental service to London. Through bookings for passengers could be made. In her new role, with the line of ports down her sides shown in this photograph, the *Natal* could accommodate fifty passengers. She ran between Freemantle and Singapore via Batavia and a number of Australian ports, and the successful service she provided led to the establishment of the West Australia Steam Navigation Company.

In 1887 the *Natal* was sold to an owner in Bangkok and for her remaining eighteen years of life she appears to have been employed in the kind of western Pacific trade so well depicted in a number of Joseph Conrad's novels. While under Philippine ownership in 1905 she went aground and became a total loss.

Deucalion 1872-1913
Iron Screw Steam Cargo Vessel

The truth of the statement that the successful operation of the *Agamemnon* and her sisters signalled the limit in time of the era of steam and sail, is illustrated by this photograph of the *Deucalion*, also an Ocean Steamship Company vessel, in the Suez Canal. She was built in 1872, only seven years after the three pioneers, but her general appearance resembles that of vessels afloat eighty years later. Although she carries two big sails set from standing gaffs on her tall masts and two headsails, these are little more than vestiges of a former era at sea and they are the result of the combination of reliable economical machinery and the Suez Canal route, eliminating long passages in areas of predictable winds. She was equipped with the same general type of compound steam engine as was the *Agamemnon* and like the former vessel she appears to have carried a number of different combinations of sail over the years, until the use of sail was finally done away with in the Ocean Steamship Company's ships in 1885.

The *Deucalion* is shown in this photograph as part of a convoy of steam vessels—all more heavily rigged than she—in the Suez Canal 'gared' to the bank to allow a convoy to pass in the

opposite direction. The opening of the canal in 1869 reduced the distance from Britain to China by 3,000 miles or ten to twelve steaming days for the vessels of the period. This was another factor in the demise of the sailing vessel in the Eastern trade, but it meant also that vessels less efficient than those developed by the Ocean Steamship Company could operate profitably in the business. To increase their competitive margin and to take advantage of the greatly increased trading opportunities, the Ocean Steamship Company therefore had nine more ships built, of which the *Deucalion* was one.

She was launched by Andrew Leslie and Company of Newcastle-upon-Tyne in 1872, of just over 2,000 tons gross with a compound engine of 250nhp built by Robert Stephens, also of Newcastle. She was sold to Dutch associates of the Ocean Steamship Company in 1896 and when this company was sold by the Ocean Steamship Company as a going concern to Norddeutscher Lloyd in 1899 she was transferred to that company. She was broken up at Shanghai in 1913.

Germanic 1874–1950

Iron Screw Steam Passenger Liner

This very unusual photograph shows a scene on board the White Star liner *Germanic* (later owned by the American Line) at sea under both steam and sail. The *Germanic* herself had a remarkable life. Twenty years after her launch she was described as 'one of the most remarkably successful steamers ever built'. Constructed of iron by Harland and Wolff in 1874, she was 455ft long and of 5,000 tons. She was driven initially by two compound engines giving her a speed of sixteen knots and with her sister the *Britannic* she was the first liner to reduce the trans-Atlantic passage to

$7\frac{1}{2}$ days. In 1889, when she was fourteen years old, she made thirteen crossings of the North Atlantic, averaging seven days, fifteen hours and twenty-one minutes. When she was seventeen years old in 1891, she improved on all her previous crossings with a passage of seven days, seven hours and thirty-seven minutes. As the historian of the North Atlantic route, Arthur Maginnis, pointed out in 1893, these speeds were maintained far more economically than the only slightly higher speeds of much larger vessels.

The *Germanic* followed the pioneer White Star liner *Oceanic* of 1870 in having her principal accommodation amidships, replacing the narrow deck-houses and high bulwarks of earlier liners with accommodation the full width of the ship with the open deck seen here above it. Thus the passenger-carrying steamship was given the profile it was to retain for 80 years. She was also the first passenger vessel to have provided forced draft ventilation, so that passengers had some control of the temperature of their cabins.

Despite her powerful and efficient machinery the *Germanic* was rigged as a four-masted barque with short pole masts each with courses, single topsails and topgallants. The mizzen mast had a standing gaff sail in place of the course and the details of the rigging of this, the brails, the outhaul, the massive sheet blocks on their bail, the topping lift and the trackway in which the foot of the sail travelled on the boom—anticipating the mast track of the Bermudan-rigged yacht by many years—are all clearly visible in this photograph.

In 1895 the *Germanic* was given triple-expansion engines and in 1903 she made her last voyage under the White Star flag from Liverpool to New York. She was then sold to the American Steamship Company and continued in the trans-Atlantic passenger service to Southampton. Later she was sold to the Dominion Line and renamed *Ottawa*, running with passengers from Liverpool to Quebec and to Montreal until 1910 when she was sold to the Ottoman American Line. In 1915 she was torpedoed and sunk in the Sea of Marmora by the British submarine *E 14* (Commander E. C. Boyle VC) but was salved and sent back to sea.

In 1920–1 she was running from Turkey to New York with passengers and it was not until 1950 that this remarkable survivor of the age of steam and sail was finally broken up.

Anchoria 1874-1922

Iron Screw Steam Passenger Liner

The *Anchoria* was built by the Barrow Shipbuilding Company in 1874 of 4,000 tons gross, 400ft long, of iron, and with a twin-cylinder compound engine. She was the first ship to be completed for the Barrow Steamship Company which was one of the many complex ramifications of the Anchor Line. She and four sisters maintained a weekly Glasgow–New York service. At this time the vessels of this fleet were amongst the largest on the regular North Atlantic run. She remained in the North Atlantic service until 1905 when she was sold to German owners. She was broken up in 1922.

In October 1886 the *Anchoria* was involved in a dramatic incident, reported in the *Shipping Gazette & Lloyd's List Weekly Summary* as follows:

ANCHORIA (s)—Halifax, Oct 11—Further details received of the accident to the *Anchoria* show that she broke her main shaft on the morning of 22 September when about 1,200 miles west of Ireland. She then proceeded under sail, but for several days refused to answer her helm. The shaft was repaired on 6 October but after working for 36 hours it again broke. When the steamer was

about a hundred miles from land on the morning of the 8th inst. Mr M'Fard, the first officer, and a volunteer crew manned one of the boats, in which they arrived at St John's. The steamer *Miranda* then went to the *Anchoria*'s assistance, but did not succeed in falling in with her. The latter meanwhile drifted helplessly towards land, and at 5 yesterday afternoon, there appearing no signs of assistance the land being judged to be only 10 miles distant, a second boat was despatched, which reached St John's during the night. The tug *Favorite* was next sent out to the *Anchoria*'s assistance and towed her safely into St John's this morning. The passengers were placed on allowance during the latter part of the voyage, but are all in good health, and they highly praise the conduct of the *Anchoria*'s officers. The steamer will repair in the St John's Dry Dock. The saloon passengers will be forwarded to Halifax in the *Miranda*.

This photograph shows the *Anchoria* lying in St John's after being towed in. The much relieved passengers line the rails and the boat and her crew with the bearded First Officer (whose name was actually McFarlane) pose for the camera in the foreground. As long as incidents of this kind occurred in an era before radio the use of sails, however vestigial, continued in merchant vessels. It was only the development of the twin screw vessel which led to their complete abandonment.

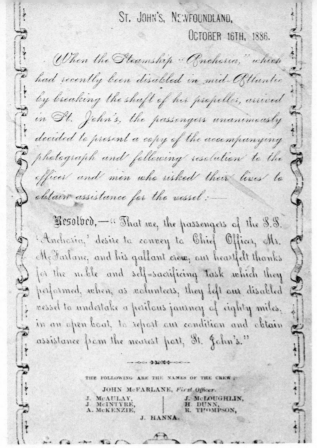

When the *Anchoria* arrived at St John's, passengers presented a copy of the photograph on the preceding page, together with the illuminated address shown in the small photograph to Mr McFarlane and his boat's crew as a demonstration of gratitude. It is to be hoped that the gratitude took a more material form as well.

Durham 1874—Converted to Sailing Vessel 1883
Iron Screw Auxiliary Steam Ship

The uneven pace at which steam was introduced for merchant ship propulsion by different companies in different trades is very clearly illustrated by the comparison of this photograph with those of the *Germanic* and the *Anchoria*. All three vessels were built in the same year. The *Germanic* was a straight-stemmed, high-sided vessel in the shape and arrangements of which can be seen the origins of the twentieth-century liner. The *Anchoria* was a full-powered steamer with sails which could do no more than assist her engines under favourable conditions or enable her to run to leeward in extreme emergency. The *Durham*, illustrated here, is a sailing ship equipped with power and differs little in external appearance from the first steam vessels in the Australian trade, like the *Calcutta*, which later spent many years as a successful sailing ship without engines.

The secret of the difference lies of course in the nature of the trades for which these vessels were constructed. The *Germanic* and the *Anchoria* were able to carry sufficient coal to make their relatively short passages between Britain and North America at full power all the time. Although it was nearly ten years since the *Agamemnon* and her sisters had shown that it was possible to operate economic full-powered steamships in long-range trades, not all shipowners had realised the finality of this demonstration. The *Durham*, built for the long run to Australia, was able to make extensive use of sail in an attempt to compete with the more heavily powered and less heavily rigged passenger steamers already sailing to the east when she was built in 1874. It has been recorded by John Malster in *North Star to Southern Cross* that many first-class passengers

in fact preferred to travel by the *Durham* and her sisters rather than by the full-powered steamships of the Peninsular & Oriental Line, which did not provide a service direct to Australia for another ten years.

The *Durham* was built of iron at Blackwall for Money Wigram and Company, a very old-established firm of London shipowners in the Indian and Australian trades. She was of 2,284 tons with a small compound engine. By the early 1880s the passenger business had finally moved away from vessels of her type and she was therefore chartered for voyages to New Zealand and Australia with cargo, the latter passage being made via the Suez Canal. After only eight years operation as a steamship the obsolete *Durham* was sold and her new owners converted her into a purely sailing vessel.

Rome 1881-1913

Iron Screw Steam Passenger Liner

The *Rome*, whose long open decks are shown here, was built of iron at Greenock in 1881 for the Peninsular & Oriental Steam Navigation Company. Of 5,000 tons gross, she had a four-cylinder tandem-compound engine but was re-engined with a triple-expansion unit in 1904 and at the same time lengthened and her tonnage increased to 5,500. She was rigged as a four-masted topsail schooner with the fore and aft sails set from standing gaffs and brailed into the masts when not set. This rig went rather oddly with a straight stem.

The *Rome* carried 160 first-class and 50 second-class passengers in accommodation of a very high standard for her period. A number of photographs of her saloons in the National Maritime Museum show comfort amounting to luxury. On her maiden voyage she inaugurated the use of Tilbury Docks as the Peninsular & Oriental home mail and passenger terminal. She continued in service on the London–Melbourne–Sydney run with intermediate calls at Indian ports until

1912, when she was converted for cruising purposes and renamed *Vectis*. She was later sold to the French government for use as a hospital ship.

The photograph should be contrasted with that of the *Germanic* on page 83. It shows very clearly the long narrow deck-houses between high bulwarks which characterised the accommodation arrangements of liners until the adoption on the North Atlantic route of the new system with the *Oceanic* of 1870. It was a number of years before the change was made in the Far Eastern passenger vessels. The photograph shows also the simplicity of the rigging of a late steam and sail liner. The main boom is fitted with foot ropes like the yards of a square-rigged ship, no doubt to make it possible to tend the trackway in which the foot of the sail presumably fitted on the boom. A seaman is fitting a cover on the furled sail. He appears to be working from a ladder built into the structure of the steel mast.

Etruria 1884-1909

Steel Screw Steam Passenger Liner

The last days of steam and sail on the North Atlantic passenger route are very well illustrated in this photograph of the Cunard liner *Etruria* built of steel in 1884 by John Elder & Co of Glasgow. She ran in the Liverpool–New York service until 1909 when she was broken up. Of 7,718 tons gross her triple-expansion engines drove one of the last single-screw vessels to be put on the North Atlantic express route. She was 500ft long and carried over 1,300 passengers, 550 in the cabin or first class, 800 in the third class. In 1892 she made an Atlantic crossing in six days and twenty minutes.

The general appearance of the *Etruria*, less her masts, the turtle deck aft, and the black smoke from her hand-fired coal-burning boilers, is really very modern. She could be mistaken for a passenger vessel in service in the 1940s. Had she had serious trouble with her single engine and screw the small sail plan would have been of use in some circumstances. Indeed, the *Etruria*'s twin sister *Umbria* probably used her sails to very good effect when she broke her thrust shaft at sea on passage to New York in 1892. Her engine-room crew repaired the shaft at sea and she completed the passage under her own steam.

As long as such incidents occurred the sails were kept in single-screw vessels though it is doubtful if they were worth their keep in normal operations. Officers whose early professional experience had been with sailing ships set them whenever they could, as on the occasion when this photograph was taken, even though there must have been little or no advantage in doing so. They probably felt it was the right thing to do and that it improved the appearance of the vessel and on this latter point they were undoubtedly right. This photograph was taken off the New England coast in 1896. Notice the barque in the background making the best of a fair wind.

C.R.R. of N.J. No 1 1892 - not known

Schooner-Rigged Coal Barge

This photograph illustrates another aspect of steam-and-sail in the sea transport of merchandise. The great trade of carrying coal to New England from Pennsylvania and Virginia was largely in the hands of very large wooden schooners until well into the twentieth century. For various reasons, notably the erratic delivery of cargoes at the loading ports, which meant that vessels were sometimes kept waiting for long periods—a kind of operation completely uneconomic for steamers—the trade remained the sailing vessel's business long after most commerce on a similar scale in North America and Europe had been taken over by powered vessels.

But there were exceptions, particularly in the anthracite industry. The Central Railroad of New Jersey carried anthracite from mines in Pennsylvania to Port Liberty, New York. Here it was loaded into vessels for distribution to all the ports in Long Island Sound and around Cape Cod as far East as Bangor in Maine. These vessels were schooner-rigged barges, built of wood on very economical lines and equipped with enough sail to help them along in a favourable wind, to steady them in a swell, and to be of use in an emergency—the role of sail in a moderately rigged steam-and-sail vessel. But in their case the steam engines were not in the barges but in big tugs which towed three barges at a time and which could perhaps get in another passage with three more barges while the first barges were being loaded or discharged. As might be imagined, these big tows were a great annoyance to other users of these narrow seas, especially in spells of fog. There is a graphic description of a meeting with one in David Livingstone's classic account of an exceptionally bad passage in an old American schooner, *Full and Bye*.

C.R.R. of N.J. No 1, like her twenty sisters, was built at Noank, Connecticut by R. Palmer & Son in 1892. She was 852 tons gross, built of wood, strengthened with diagonal iron straps. She is shown deep-laden near South Station, Boston in 1904. Astern of her is a pretty little local ferry steamer.

Special purpose vessels

Iceland 1872-1910

Wooden Screw Whaler and Sealer

In the mid-nineteenth century the United States whaling industry was at its peak and whalers from Nantucket and later New Bedford were to be found all over the world, but particularly in the Pacific. The British had pioneered the Pacific whale fishery, but they did not pursue and develop it. Their relatively small industry concentrated on the Arctic fishery for the Greenland whale. Instead of being away for years on end, like the New Bedford whalers, the British vessels hunted in the short Arctic summer, usually in the seas of northern Canada. In the second half of the century they often also made a spring voyage to Newfoundland and there joined in the slaughter of seals on the ice drifting down in the Labrador current. So close were the associations between St John's and the British whaling industry that a number of the British-built whalers were owned and registered in Newfoundland, then, of course, a British colony.

In New England the sailing whaler persisted until the 1920s. But in the British short-range Arctic fishery, conducted often in pack ice, the advantages of steam were so great that by 1865 the sailing whaler was already obsolete. She had been replaced by a type of wooden barque- or barquentine-rigged steamer, using sails to approach the whales because the noise of the screw frightened them, using steam in the ice, and steam and sail together on the passage across the Atlantic. These rigged wooden steamers were among the most handsome and commercially successful of all later steam and sail merchant vessels. Because of their enormous strength—their

frames were sometimes so close together as to be almost solid—until the advent of big ice breakers in the mid-twentieth century they remained the best kind of vessel (except for specially-built ships like the Norwegian *Fram* or the Canadian *Arctic*) for ice navigation. Consequently, a number of them were used by explorers, most notably Captain Scott, Sir Ernest Shackleton, Sir Douglas Mawson and Admiral Byrd.

The vessel in the photograph is the steam barquentine *Iceland* built in Dundee by Alexander Stephen & Son in 1872 and owned by John Munn & Company of St John's, Newfoundland, where she was registered. She was 150ft long and fitted with a twin-cylinder engine built by Pearce Brothers of Dundee quoted as being of 90hp. She is shown discharging seal pelts at Harbour Grace, Newfoundland, after her first sealing voyage. She was lost in the ice north east of Funk Island off the Newfoundland coast in 1910.

The small print shows one of the most successful of all steam and sail whalers, the *Eclipse*, built at Aberdeen in 1866 and photographed in her natural habitat, the Canadian Arctic, from the Canadian exploration ship *Arctic* in 1906.

The Steam Sealers

When the Greenland whale became greatly reduced in numbers, probably as a result of the overkilling of young whales and females, the British Arctic whaling industry died out, shortly before World War I. Many of the steam-and-sail whalers continued to operate under Newfoundland ownership in the annual seal hunt from St John's and Harbour Grace. In this industry they made one dangerous voyage into the ice each year and since the use of their sails was less important than in the whale fishery they worked under reduced canvas, using only staysails and a few squaresails on the foremast. These 'wooden walls of Newfoundland' as they became known, were the world's last regularly employed steam-and-sail merchant vessels and

they continued to earn their living in the seal hunt until World War II.

The photograph was taken long before these last days and shows a fleet of steam sealers in the ice viewed from the stern of one of them. This sort of scene continued off the Newfoundland coast until the beginning of the 1930s. The sealing industry and the life around it in the days of the wooden steam sealers is graphically described in a delightful book *The Wooden Walls Among the Ice Floes* by Major W. Howe Green, one of the best accounts of a specialised form of seafaring ever published.

The small print shows the steam whaler and sealer *Terra Nova* owned in St John's lying in St John's harbour shortly before her last voyage in the early 1940s. This was probably the last photograph ever taken of her. She was lost in the ice off the Greenland coast shortly afterwards. The *Terra Nova* was world famous in her generation as the vessel which was used by Captain Robert Falcon Scott on the expedition to the South Pole in 1910 which resulted in the heroic deaths of himself and his companions. She was built at Dundee in 1884 and was twice bought for work in the Antarctic, returning afterwards to her sealing work from St John's, Newfoundland.

Vanguard 1873-1909

Wood Screw Steam Sealer

The *Vanguard* was built by Alexander Hall & Company at Aberdeen in 1873. A barque-rigged steamship of 559 tons gross, she was old fashioned at such a late date in having the deep single topsails which in general had passed out of favour by the end of the 1860s. As the photograph shows, she was an unusually handsome vessel with a very nice balance of lines, masts, funnel and charthouse. Her engine, of 85nhp, was essential to her in her lifetime of work in the Newfoundland sealing industry. In 1897 she was badly damaged while trying to force her way through exceptionally thick ice and in April 1909 she was finally lost while sealing off the east coast of Newfoundland.

Note the open bridge which straddles the poop between the funnel and the mizzenmast. The vessel is steered with an open wheel in the extreme stern, sailing ship fashion. The charthouse is immediately forward of the funnel and the small house with a tall chimney immediately forward of the break of the poop is the galley. The very long topgallant forecastle was to accommodate the large crews of seal hunters carried in this trade. The vessel's own working crew was relatively small. For much of her career the *Vanguard* probably worked with no yards on her mainmast and perhaps no topgallant on the fore.

94

H.M.S. *later* USS *Alert 1856-95*

Wooden Screw Steam Sloop—Exploration Ship

The *Alert* was built at Pembroke Dockyard in 1856 as a sloop for the British Navy and engined at Chatham Dockyard. She was a wooden full-rigged ship 160ft long with a low-power steam engine and was armed with seventeen thirty-two pounder smooth-bore guns, eight in each broadside and one as a bow chaser. Too late for the Crimean War, her interesting and most unusual career began when, already 18 years old, she was refitted for the British naval attempt to reach the North Pole in 1875–6. Her hull was sheathed over with additional planking, she was rigged as a barque and equipped with a compound engine by Hawthorn, quoted as of 312 nominal horsepower, capable of driving her at about $7\frac{1}{2}$ knots on 6 tons per day of best ordinary Welsh coal.

Accompanied for most of the time by the *Discovery*, a barque-rigged steam whaler commissioned as a naval vessel, she sailed between the east coast of what is now the Canadian archipelago and the west coast of Greenland, to 82° 27′ North. There she wintered in the most northerly position ever reached by any European vessel to that date, a record not equalled in this sector of the Arctic for very many years.

After this adventure she was employed as a survey vessel in Canadian and Australian waters and it was during this stage of her career that the photograph was taken. But in 1884 her career took a yet more unusual turn in that she was transferred from the British to the United States Navy to play a part under Captain George W. Coffin, USN in the rescue of the Greely Expedition. After the completion of this operation she was transferred to the Canadian Government

95

service and employed on survey work in Hudson Bay. As a British naval vessel she had originally carried 175 officers and men. On her first Arctic voyage she had carried 61. On Canadian survey voyages in 1885 and 1886 she had a crew of 32 and 17 technical officers. As a result of these survey voyages, Lieutenant A. R. Gordon, her captain, recommended Churchill as the appropriate site for the terminus of a Hudson Bay railway and his opinion was to be justified by the opening of the port for regular deep-sea trade nearly fifty years later.

USCGC *Bear 1874–1963*

Wooden Screw Steam Sealer, Coastguard Cutter and Exploration Ship

The steam barquentine *Bear* was launched by Alexander Stephen and Sons, Dundee in 1874 as a Newfoundland sealer. She was the twenty-ninth steam sealer to enter the trade. Of 688 tons gross and with an engine of 101 nominal horse power, she was owned by Walter Grieve & Company of St John's, Newfoundland. In 1884 she was sold to the United States Government to take part with the *Alert* (qv) and the *Thetis*, another Newfoundland sealer, in the search for the lost Lt A. W. Greely of the United States Army and his party in the Arctic. They were known to be starving to death because relief supply ships had been unable to reach them in the summer of 1883. The relief expedition carried in the *Bear* and the other vessels was successful in rescuing Greely himself and six other survivors.

On her return to the USA the *Bear* was commissioned as a cutter of the Revenue Marine. From 1885 until 1915 she sailed in this capacity on annual patrols in Alaskan waters and it was about the middle of this period that the photograph was taken. These were years of great activity in this area, with whaling, sealing and gold-seeking all being conducted with the inevitable consequence that the *Bear* was involved in numerous rescue and law-keeping missions. In 1915 she was absorbed into the newly formed United States Coast Guard and she continued on the Arctic patrol until 1926 when she was laid up, eventually to become a marine museum at Oakland, California.

In 1932 she began a new seagoing life when she acted as second vessel for Admiral Byrd's second Antarctic Expedition and spent two summers in the Ross Sea. On her return to the United

States in 1935 she was again laid up but was recommissioned in 1939 for another Antarctic Expedition. She was re-masted, re-rigged and re-engined with diesels. During World War II, once more a coastguard cutter, she made the first United States naval capture of the war when her crew arrested the German ship *Baskor*. After the war she was sold and laid up in Halifax for fifteen years. In 1963 she avoided the fate of becoming a floating restaurant by sinking while under tow at the age of 89.

Nimrod 1866-1919

Wooden Screw Steam Sealer

The steam sealer *Nimrod* was built by Alexander Stephen & Son at Dundee in 1866 for Job Brothers, the prominent Newfoundland merchants. She was one of the smallest of the steam-and-sail whaler type of vessel, only 136ft long, barquentine-rigged but with her funnel between the mainmast and the foremast so that a full gaff and boom mainsail could be carried without lowering the funnel. With the funnel in this position the normal staysails of a barquentine would have been blackened by smoke and burned by the heat from the furnace, so the *Nimrod* had a gaff and boom sail on the fore lower mast for at least part of her career. She had a two-cylinder engine quoted as being of 60hp. As to the sort of assistance such an engine gave, after a long voyage in another small steam sealer a contemporary wrote, 'When sailing five knots, slow ahead with the engine would add about one and a half knots to the speed of our heavy vessel: sailing seven to eight knots, the propeller was of little assistance'.

Nimrod carried the British explorer Lieutenant, later Sir Ernest, Shackleton to the Antarctic in 1907 on what was to be an almost successful attempt to reach the South Pole. During this voyage she proved herself an admirable vessel for the purpose, given the limitations of the technology of the period. She never returned to Canada and to sealing but after a period laid up she was employed as a cargo-carrying vessel in British waters. She was lost on the Barber Sand off Caister, Norfolk, in January 1919 when carrying a cargo of coal. The photograph shows her in Falmouth as an exploration ship. Lying alongside her are a small steam launch and one of the watermen's sailing boats of the type locally known as a quay punt.

Discovery 1900 - Still Afloat

Wooden Screw Steam Exploration Ship

The British research ship *Discovery* was built by the Dundee Shipbuilding Company in 1900. She was commissioned by the Ship Committee established to provide a vessel for the National Antarctic Expedition which was to be under the command of Commander (later Captain) R. F. Scott. She was designed by W. E. Smith, at that time Chief Naval Constructor, to quote Captain Scott himself 'more or less on the lines of' an earlier vessel of the same name, the steam-and-sail whaler which had been the consort of the *Alert* (qv) on her great voyage in the Canadian Arctic. 172ft long, the barque-rigged *Discovery* was massively built of wood to stand the buffeting and the strains of prolonged work in pack ice. She was equipped with a lifting propeller and as a safeguard against damage in ice the rudder also lifted up through the deck. She had a triple-expansion engine built by Gourlay Brothers of Dundee designed to give 450ihp, which in fact delivered over 500hp on trials. She was therefore a very heavily powered vessel of her type.

The reason for the use of steam-and-sail vessels for exploration purposes was, of course, their long range. With care they could operate for several years away from home even though the fuel of the period was steam coal which was bulky to store and awkward to handle, by using their engines only when necessary in the ice.

The National Antarctic Expedition was one of the most successful of several from different European countries at the time which marked a renaissance of interest in the southern continent after many years of total neglect. This renaissance has culminated in the great United States

Operation Deep Freeze with its permanent stations near the *Discovery*'s wintering place at Ross Island and at the South Pole. After she returned to Britain the *Discovery* became a merchant ship sailing for the Hudson's Bay Company but she was subsequently employed in Antarctic research work again. Much altered from her original form she is still afloat, lying in the Thames in the heart of London as Headquarters Ship of the London Division of the Royal Naval Reserve. Although she has no engine, in external appearance she is one of the few steam-and-sail vessels left afloat. It is to be hoped that she can be preserved indefinitely, preferably with her yards restored, although it must be remembered that, like many vessels of her class, she spent years of her working life only partly rigged.

The first photograph shows her on her trials in the Tay in 1901. Note the paddle tug which bears a close resemblance to the National Maritime Museum's *Reliant*. The paddle tug was a very significant factor in later nineteenth-century merchant ship development, virtually making possible the development of the big sailing ship. The second photograph shows a scene on the bridge during trials.

Wooden Screw Steam Exploration Ship

The resurgence of interest in the Antarctic, which was manifested in Britain by the *Discovery* Expedition of 1901–4, found expression in Germany in the building in 1900 of the *Gauss*, also a wooden steam and sail vessel but of very different design. The *Gauss* was not a full-bodied merchant ship in shape but was designed with a great rise of floor so that under pressure from sea ice she would be squeezed above it. This general form had proved itself in the steam schooner *Fram*, still preserved at Oslo, in which the great Norwegian explorer Nansen had made his epic voyage nearest the North Pole in the 1890s. The *Gauss* was built by Howaldstwerke at Kiel, 165ft long with a triple-expansion engine of 44nhp. She was rigged as a barquentine.

After an Antarctic voyage the *Gauss* was sold in 1904 to the Canadian government and her subsequent history is entirely North American. As the *Arctic* she made a series of voyages north of the North American continent which played a large part in establishing Canadian sovereignty and administration over the Arctic archipelago. This was a development of great long-term political significance, not only for Canada and the United States, but for the whole world during

the period of 'cold war'. On these voyages she was commanded by Captain Joseph Bernier, one of the great figures in North America Arctic history, in what has been described as the penultimate exposition of the heroic school of personal leadership and small wooden ships—the ultimate being the circling of the North American continent by Larsen in the motor and sail schooner *St Roch*. On these long voyages the *Arctic*'s efficiency was greatly increased by the big coal supply she could carry, which was over 500 tons, 165 tons more than the *Discovery* with her larger engine, and this meant that the *Arctic* could stay for two years in the ice if necessary.

The photograph shows her leaving Quebec at the outset of an Arctic voyage on 28 July 1906. In the background is a typical Canadian tern schooner, a three-master with all her masts of the same height.

The first small print was taken on board the *Arctic* in July 1910. It will be noted that no sails are set from the vessel's mainmast. With a barquentine rig, a steam and sail vessel could not use sail on her mainmast while steaming because the funnel blocked the working of the main boom. A solution lay in placing the machinery amidships and the funnel abaft the foremast, as in the sealer *Nimrod*. The second small print shows the lifting screw of the *Fram*, mentioned above. The *Arctic* had a similar device which was a development of the lifting screws of the steam and sail merchant vessels of the 1850s.

Chunar 1845-79

Iron Paddle Steam River Cargo Vessel

This unique painting shows the Indian river steamer *Chunar*, a side-paddle vessel with a mast and topmast from which squaresails were set. She belonged to the Ganges Company, a British concern operating cargo services on the Ganges in India with five steamers. In 1867 this Company was merged with the India General Steam Navigation Company.

The story of the river steamer fleets of the Ganges and the Brahmaputra has been neglected, but they played a large part in the development of eastern India and what is now Bangla Desh. In a country in which other forms of communication are impossible, because the land is broken up by a maze of waterways, they provided the transport which permitted the development of the tea industry in Assam and Bengal and of the jute-growing industry in East Bengal. Without them it is doubtful if the British would have been able to adopt Indian tea as their national drink.

With her use of steam-and-sail the *Chunar* was typical of the early steamers on the great rivers, which in places are as much as ten miles wide. But well before the end of the century with the introduction of reliable compound engines the masts and sails were given up, and in due course the steamers acquired a second deck so that they were like great two-storey houses. A number of paddle steamers are still in use on the rivers of Bangla Desh.

The *Chunar* was lost in 1879 when she was leaving Calcutta in bad weather. A steering gear chain parted and she went aground and broke up.

Sunbeam, 1874-1929

Composite Screw Steam Yacht

The *Sunbeam*, a three-masted standing topgallant steam schooner, was designed to perform equally well under steam or sail. 170ft long, setting nearly 8,500sq ft of canvas at the maximum, equipped with an engine delivering 350ihp and a feathering propeller, she can be taken as a classic great yacht of the steam and sail era. Owned for many years by Lord Brassey she became world famous, even in her day when there were many such large privately owned vessels, for the extent of her ocean voyaging. Many of her early passages were recorded by the first Lady Brassey and published in a series of books by her which were best sellers in their time and still make excellent reading. In 1876 and 1877 the *Sunbeam* was taken round the world and is believed to have been only the second steam yacht to complete a circumnavigation. She visited Australia in 1887, the West Indies and the United States in 1892 and India again in 1893-4. She made many more long passages in the following years until 1914.

Like the biggest merchant schooners in the Newfoundland trade, which she closely resembled in outward appearance, the *Sunbeam* was an excellent performer off the wind or with the wind on the beam, though by modern standards a poor performer to windward. She was a very safe vessel, excellently manned and run by a highly professional crew, in early years drawn principally from Essex, later from the Westcountry. After serving as a hospital ship she passed into the hands of the Government of India after World War I. She was subsequently bought by the first Lord

Runciman and owned by him and his family for extensive cruising until, worn out, she was broken up in 1929.

The *Sunbeam* and her voyages may be taken as a supreme example of what was meant by grand yachting at its Victorian and Edwardian best. In some ways, socially, technically, and in her highly skilled close-knit crews of professional seamen drawn from a limited area, she represents the best aspects of her period. Many of the sail training ships which take part in the Tall Ships Races today are modern equivalents of the *Sunbeam* and her contemporaries, rather than of the sailing merchant ships of the same period.

Waterlily 1876

Wooden Screw Steam Yacht

The elegant small steam yacht was one of the most characteristic features of late Victorian and Edwardian yachting centres. These vessels had small compound engines with hand-fired coal-burning boilers and required an engineer and stokehold crew of three or four in addition to deck hands, mate, master, cook and stewards. They were frequently schooner-rigged and they had clipper bows, figureheads and long bowsprits with jibbooms over them. Photographs of such vessels at anchor are common, but pictures of yachts of this type under sail are quite rare.

Of the various yachts named *Waterlily* or *Water Lily* at the time this photograph was taken in the 1890s, it seems most likely that the vessel depicted is an auxiliary schooner built by Day and Summers (who had built the *Natal* [qv] ten years before) in 1876. Equipped with a two-cylinder compound engine built by J. S. White of Cowes, described as of 78hp, she was about 120ft long.

The last days of steam-and-sail

Lieutenant Garnier 1918
Wooden Screw Steam Cargo Vessel

Except for special purposes, such as the Newfoundland sealing industry and for polar exploration, the use of low-powered steam ships equipped with sails, of sails as an auxiliary for high-powered steamers and of steam engines as auxiliary to sails in sailing vessels had virtually ceased in Britain and North America by World War I. But during that war the acute shortage of tonnage resulted in the building of a number of vessels whose construction was dictated by demand and the availability of materials. These included a few wooden sailing vessels with steam auxiliary machinery which were built in North America, including the large five-masted wooden schooners *Lieutenant Garnier*, *Lieutenant Delorme* and *Lieutenant Pegoud* launched by the Foundation Company of Portland, Oregon, for the French Government in 1918. They were of identical dimensions, each almost 260ft long and equipped with twin triple-expansion engines of 68 nominal horsepower, built by J. W. Sullivan of New York. They had twin funnels, one on each side of the jigger mast. Though like many big American schooners the *Lieutenant Garnier* must have been an economical and efficient cargo carrier in some trades, rapid improvement of the economic and efficient marine diesel engines meant that experiments of this kind were not repeated after 1918, and steam-and-sail became motor and sail. A number of large merchant vessels designed to operate under sail and diesel power—like the German five-masted schooners *Carl*, *Adolph*, *Werner*,

Christel and *Susanne Vinnen*, built at Kiel for F. A. Vinnen and Co of Hamburg in the early 1920s—remained in commercial operation for many years until further technical advances made the commercial use of sail at sea finally obsolete. But it was a long process.

Many motor and sail schooners and ketches were built in Sweden, Denmark, Spain, Portugal, the Soviet Union, the West Indies and elsewhere until the middle of the present century and some of these vessels are still in use in different parts of the world.

The first small print shows a British survivor, the steam ketch *Echo* built by J. D. Foster at Emsworth, Hampshire, in 1902 for oyster and scallop dredging on voyages which took her as far away as the Spanish coast. She was 112ft long, one of the largest British sail-using fishing vessels, and she remained at work at sea until 1936. The second shows an Estonian steamer, rigged as a two-masted schooner with standing gaffs, brailing sails and booms used as cargo booms, which one of the authors photographed discharging cargo in Dover as late as 1939. The third shows the German five-masted steel diesel schooner *Carl Vinnen* photographed by one of the authors in the Kattegat in 1937, and the fourth a Swedish steel motor schooner photographed in the English Channel in 1948.

Hussar 1931 - Still Afloat

Steel Screw Diesel Four-Masted Barque Yacht

This vessel should not strictly be included in this book, for despite her appearance she is in fact driven by diesel engines. But although she was built in 1931 she is in the grandest tradition of steam-and-sail. As such we feel she belongs here, more so since she is still in use at sea and conveys today something of the impression which the heavily rigged screw steamers of the 1840s and 1850s like the *Great Britain* must have made on those who saw them at sea.

Launched at Kiel by Friedrich Krupp, the *Antarna* as she is now called was the last four-masted barque ever to be built and one of the few vessels of this rig ever to be equipped with a main skysail. She was built for an American owner, E. F. Hutton, of New York and she was first named *Hussar*. She had accommodation for a complement, crew and guests, of sixty. Her four diesels developed about 6,000hp.

Built as a luxurious private yacht, the *Hussar* soon became the *Sea Cloud* and as such she spent years in European waters before World War II. During the war she was operated by the US Coastguard and after it she became the yacht of the President of the Dominican Republic, under the name *Angelita*. In 1963 she became a cruise ship, again owned in the United States but under the Panamanian flag. She was renamed *Patria* and, after being extensively refitted in Italy in 1968, in 1969 she was again making charter cruises out of Miami, Florida, now named *Antarna*.

Short Reading List
Warships

In many respects, much the best account of most of the ships of the Royal Navy coming within our category is given in the articles by Admiral G. A. Ballard, CB, which appeared frequently in *Mariner's Mirror*, the quarterly journal of the Society for Nautical Research, between 1929 and 1940, and thereafter at longer intervals until 1949.

Capt S. Eardley-Wilmot. *The Development of Navies* (Seeley Service, 1892)

Parkes, Oscar. *British Battleships* (Seeley Service, 1957)

Preston, A. and Major, J. *Send a Gunboat* (Seeley Service, 1967)

Robertson, Eng Cdr F. L. *The Evolution of Naval Armament* (1921)

Smith, CBE, Eng Capt E. C. *A Short History of Marine Engineering* (Cambridge, 1937)

For ships of the United States Navy:

Bennet, Frank M. *The Steam Navy of the United States* (Pittsburg, 1896) deals with the ships of our period from an engineer's point of view.

Chapelle, Howard I. *The History of the American Sailing Navy* (1949) gives useful information on the transition to steam.

Sprout, Harold and Margaret. *The Rise of American Naval Power 1776–1918* (Princeton, 1939) provides a good survey of general policy.

Very, Lt E. W. *Navies of the World* (1880) describes the American ships of his time in relation to those of other countries as a line officer who was on the board that considered the first ships of the new United States Navy.

S. E. Morison's *Old Bruin*, a biography of M. C. Perry, A. Mahan's *Farragut*, and the autobiographies of Admirals George Dewey and Robley D. Evans throw a clear light on the personalities who handled and fought these fine ships.

Merchant and Special Purpose Vessels

Body, Geoffrey. *British Paddle Steamers* (Newton Abbot, 1971) provides a very useful account of the development of the steamship.

Garrard, Apsley Cherry. *The Worst Journey in the World* (London 1937) has a very good narrative of the outward voyage of the *Terra Nova* to the Antarctic in 1910, which describes many aspects of the operation of a steam and sail vessel on a long ocean voyage.

Greene, Major W. Howe. *The Wooden Walls among the Ice Floes* (London, 1933) contains an admirable account of the Newfoundland seal fishery.

Greenhill, Basil and Giffard, Ann. *Travelling by Sea in the Nineteenth Century* (London, 1972) is a collaboration by one of the authors containing a summary of the development of the passenger ship in the steam and sail era with a good deal of information about what it was like to travel in them.

Lubbock, Basil. *The Arctic Whalers* (Glasgow, 1968) is the best account of the British steam and sail whaling industry.

Rowland, K. T. *Steam at Sea* (Newton Abbot, 1970) and *The Great Britain* (Newton Abbot, 1971) are useful accounts of steamship development generally and of the *Great Britain* in particular.

Acknowledgements

All photographs are from the National Maritime Museum Historic Photographs Collection, except for the United States ships noted below. The original photographs following came to the museum from the sources gratefully acknowledged here:

Warships

Warrior	Imperial War Museum
Captain (large photograph)	Imperial War Museum
Volage (both photographs)	Imperial War Museum
Raleigh (large photograph)	Imperial War Museum
Imperieuse	Imperial War Museum
USS *Chicago*	Imperial War Museum
Raleigh (small photograph)	Mr H. C. Willis, Simon's Town Historical Society
Sparrowhawk	Canadian Armed Forces
Charybdis	Canadian Armed Forces
Egeria	Canadian Armed Forces
Cormorant	Canadian Armed Forces
Amphion	Canadian Armed Forces
Shearwater	Canadian Armed Forces

Ships of the United States Navy

The authors are indebted to the Naval History Division, United States Navy, for the following photographs and permission to reproduce them:

Mississippi
Powhatan
Florida
Vandalia (both photographs)
Kearsarge
Brooklyn
Atlanta

They also thank Captain C. H. H. Owen RN, for assisting to select them. The photograph of the USS *Franklin* is reproduced by permission of the Maritime Photo Library.

Merchant Ships

Iris	Maritime Museum, Elsinore, Denmark
Gipsy	Reece Winstone
Anchoria	Anchor Line
Steam Sealers	Public Archives of Canada
Bear	Mariner's Museum, Newport News, USA
Arctic (small photograph)	Public Archives of Canada

The authors wish to thank especially Robin Craig of University College London, editor of the journal *Maritime History*, and David W. Waters, Keeper at the National Maritime Museum, for their constructive criticism and suggestions.

Index